What Happened to Dad?

Tom McGraw

Copyright © 2016

ISBN:0692799923
ISBN-13:9780692799925

DEDICATION

To my children Tommy, Brooklyn, Sydney, Savonna, Colby, you are the arrows in my quiver.

I had always heard about those who had "found" God, but I didn't think it was anything more than an ascension of the mind. A decision made by an individual to change for the better. But for The Creator to suddenly take over someone's life for SEEMINGLY no reason at all and fill them with undeniable joy? This I never even knew to be possible!

The life changes that I have experienced have produced the kind of feelings I expected to have immediately following my baptism, but didn't. Now here I am some seven years past that ceremony and it has finally hit me. But why so "out of the blue" and why now? I can really only speculate, but I'm guessing it's for you.

What has happened to me *PROVES* that God is real however, and I want you to never forget that. So I wrote this book for you, my children, because it will be rough at times and you may need reminding.

"I have said these things to you, that in me you may have peace. In the world you will have tribulation. But take heart; I have overcome the world."

John 16:33

CONTENTS

ACKNOWLEDGMENTS

To my wife who has been nothing short of a miracle placed in just the
right place at just the right time, thank you Heidi, I will praise God
endlessly for you and your enduring love.
And a special thank you to Denny Scott for helping me make sense of
this journal so that I can tell of my witness of God's great grace and
mercy for us all.

SOME ORIGINAL JOURNAL ENTRIES

ORIGINAL JOURNAL ENTRIES

5-21-14

Wow, what a day! I've never felt so perfect in all my life! Everything has been enhanced 10 fold it seems. My senses are heightened to the max. Tastes are even better and I thought it wasn't possible.

Putting in lower path and really enjoying life! Having lunch-

Everything makes more sense than ever before. It's as if the puzzle has been put together today....

5-22-14

It's still here! Not filling me up- but here. I've been compelled to get up @ 4:30 over the last few days, (several actually), and have a few hours of quiet time to myself-HUGE!

5-23-14

I'm completely filled with joy today- I came downstairs and had a cup of coffee and checked the news then began editing and writing in my journal. The more I recall and write the better and more mentally coordinated I feel.

Lots to do today so better get to it. Will study Bible later.

1

WHO I WAS

Is God real? Is there really a supreme being that created Heaven and earth and everything in between? These questions used to exist in my mind, my child, but not anymore. Not since Arizona. What you are about to read is a no punches pulled account of how the Holy Spirit has been poured out to me by God, which was and continues to be nothing short of miraculous. I say "no punches pulled" because it is very raw. I wanted to keep it as original as possible so I did very little editing. I hope you can forgive my writing ignorance and stay the course because it will be more than worth it in the end.

I originally didn't write this with anything in mind other to be able to reflect back on it one day and figure out what had happened, but then it just grew into something much bigger. It grew like, well, the mustard seed, (you'll have to read the parable of the mustard seed if you aren't sure what I mean).

As you know, I am NOT by trade a writer or theologian. You should also know that I am not a self proclaimed evangelist or looking to "save" you, (or anyone for that matter). In fact, I now know by what has happened to me that only God can *really* save. After all, no one did or said anything to me to begin my process of salvation, at least, that is, within the span of time that it actually began. But maybe the seed was planted long ago. For this reason I have included a few chapters of my earliest spiritual history. Plus, I know I would have liked to know more about **my** dad's early history, and I figure you might be just a bit like me, so I threw some in. This insight into who I was will also serve as a contrast to who it is God has changed me into.

As you also know, outside of being a former professional baseball player with a few days played at the major league level, I am really just a "normal" human being. There is really nothing special about me, but, for reasons only known by God, I've been transformed from the inside out. But why? This is what this is truly all about, why me and why now? In my confused state I said that a lot, so please bear with me on that as well.

You have to understand this first and foremost. when this first started happening I didn't have even the slightest idea what was going on, it was all happening so fast and decisively and I felt like I didn't have a choice. Thankfully for the sake of my sanity, I have since received many revelations to help explain what was happening, the most recent of which has at least explained to me what I have become and who I now am.

I know now according to scripture that I am one of His elect, a bond slave to Him. I know this to be true because I wake every day wanting to do only His will, and I absolutely love it! I am a witness to His awesome power and I have no choice but to witness to anyone The Father brings my way. My cup is truly overflowing with His love!

Although awesome and beautiful, and even sometimes supernatural, my transformation hasn't been easy, however. This new life has come with many challenges, some much more profoundly

difficult than others. I now know what He meant
when Jesus said that He did not come to bring peace,
but division in Luke 12:51,(I suggest you look that
one up as well).

Anyway, let's get on with it shall we? I very
truly hope that from reading this you can understand
that our God is a great and awesome God and that
He loves you even more than I do.

2

SHAPING THE CLAY

Having been adopted at birth I've never known my biological parents, nor have I ever really wanted to. My older sister, older brother and I were placed by God into a loving, middle class family. My mother and father, your Grandma Judy and Grandpa Phil, raised us on ten acres out in the country. I grew up on a small farm that consisted of a small herd of cattle, a barnyard full of chickens and ducks and one turkey that would chase us kids whenever we got too close. We also raised some pigs from time to time which all helped to keep our grocery bill to a minimum. We weren't able to have much in the way of extras but I don't ever recall going to bed hungry or going to school without what we needed to fit in or participate in athletics, my Grandpa and Grandma made sure of that. I can't tell you the number of times that we made the forty-five minute drive to Portland to visit Na Na and Pop, (as we called them), but whenever we did we came home with more more then we went with. They not only gave us money whenever we needed help, but vehicle help as well. Pop had more mechanical knowledge than anyone I've ever known and was as clever as they came. I loved him and my Na Na very, very much.

My earliest recollection of a religious upbringing took place at the local church about a half mile away, on the highest hill around. Our church is as picturesque as they come for a small town. It's small and simple white box construction is straight out of a Norman Rockwell painting. The double door entrance walks you through the steeple which contains a bell that could be heard ringing throughout the valley each and every Sunday.

The community I called home consisted of

one four way stop and one tiny store about an eighth of a mile from our house that my brother and sister could walk to for a treat if we were "good". I still recall the store owner, Mr. Jiggs, playfully popping me on the top of my head with the bottom of the paper bag in the act of opening it whenever we bought something. It was as small town as it gets and looking back now I realize just how blessed I was.

Why my parents dropped us off but didn't attend with us I still don't know to this day but it seemed just fine to us at the time. It was probably as simple as just giving them, and us kids a much needed break. I never saw it as a negative and I still don't. Which denomination we were I couldn't tell you, but this was my first recollection of learning about God.

I still feel regret about how I acted during services. As young, unsupervised boys, more then once my brother and I had started the service in the back pew by our choice but later wound up being moved to the front by the preacher's choice. I guess church was, to my brother and I, a chance to test our newly formed boundaries of freedom.

As I remember it, we did one immature thing after another. From finger flicking battles that escalated into shoulder bruising wars to uncontrolled giggling fits, the reasons for being brought to front and center varied from Sunday to Sunday. I have since seen my first pastor Larry, and given him and his wife Carolyn my most sincere apologies, which they simply smiled at and accepted, as any good Christian would.

My next spiritual "growth" took place in and around the 4th grade. My best friend's father was the preacher at the local Baptist church so I became involved in those services as well as in their youth group, I recall really enjoying the journey, that is until the bonfire experience.

This "fun-loving" bonfire was initially advertised to us kids as a nighttime spiritual get together and I recall being very excited to go. I mean what gradeschooler wouldn't love to watch a giant controlled burn? I pictured a marsh mellow/wienie roasting, God loving gathering, that is until I was made aware of the kindling that would be used to start it. Our youth director went on to explain that we should all bring our rock and roll tapes, comic books, baseball cards, and anything else that we "idolized." Naturally, without any further explanation, this came off as quite strange to me, but I remember keeping quiet about it. But as time went on, the question of 'why?' kept nagging at my brain, and finally I couldn't take it any longer so I asked. I remember the director looking me straight in the eye and, with a devilish smile, responding with the words I feared most. "We're going to burn them little buddy."

Now you gotta understand, my brother and I were avid and competitive comic book collectors and I also collected sports cards. These were more than just cardboard pictures, they held pictures of my heroes. And on top of that, I had worked hard doing my chores around the farm to earn the money to buy those comics and football cards.

Well, I decided right then and there that I would not be going to that bonfire. In fact, I didn't go to that church, not one more time. My father painted the 4x8 plywood backdrop of Mt. St. Helens for the baptismal in which I had earlier received my first Baptism, but that didn't matter. I knew in my heart that I wanted nothing to do with a church that was taking away my hard earned treasures and therefore a piece of my freedom as well. I believe that this is when my rejection of God began, not a complete denial, but I began to see Him in a less than positive light, that's for sure.

Due to the short-sightedness of the leaders of that church, God's love for me changed into something that had to be earned and from that point forward I saw the church as something that stood between me and a good time. As I look back now, it was actually from that point on that I began to viewed God as a hindrance and a rebel was born.

All throughout my childhood and much of my early adult years I harbored a rebelliousness that would bubble up from time to time. It was never so strong as to get me into serious trouble, but it existed nonetheless. From intentionally causing waves in grade school by wearing an obscene t-shirt to paying a $20 fine with a sack full of quarters in the minor leagues for not wearing my uniform "the right way", I guess there were times it just needed to come out.

Although I somewhat prided myself on my sporadic rebellious "bad boy" existence, I was never a bad person. I must admit, however, I've always taken great pleasure in dominating the cocky types, athletically that is, so they may have a differing opinion about me from back in those days. But off the field I was as fun loving a spirit as there was. If there was an argument or fight at a after game party, I was usually the one keeping the peace with a cold beer diversion. Being from very simple family life I was taught early on by my father to always be humble and loyal. I can still hear my dad tell me to let my actions do the talking. I was also taught to treat others how I wanted to be treated and that family and team were always first. My friends and family meant everything to me, just as they do today. If anyone needed help in any way, I did what needed to be done.

Throughout my early 80's high school years I admired and longed for the rock star lifestyle. I gravitated toward older peers because of my athletic talent and a self esteem based on my ability to play the game of baseball and party with the "big boys" flourished. My ego had taken on a life of it's own and, I began traveling down what I now know was a self destructive road, although it didn't feel like it at the time . All evidence led me to believe that I was special, and I guess I wanted to show that to everyone by being a success despite leading an anti All-American lifestyle. The rebel in me wanted to prove I could be an All-American and not live the All-American life. I had thrown no-hitters, hit game winning grand slams and won many ego building accolades living this way. There were times when I felt untouchable by anyone or anything. I was athletically talented and seemingly unstoppable, destined to make millions of dollars doing what I loved, playing the game of baseball. Life was so sweet and simple. Too sweet and simple.

I went on to fall in love with my high school sweetheart and promise my mother the house she had always wanted, an 'A' frame with big windows. Despite my use of drugs and alcohol my grades didn't suffer throughout high school. I also enjoyed great success playing the game, which only fueled my thoughts of invincibility, so the party raged on. It wasn't until college that the good times began to affect my grades, but even that didn't matter. In my mind I would be hiring someone to do my accounting, why should I learn about it?

Then came my first real setback.

During my college sophomore season I suffered a shoulder injury and surgery was required to repair it. My indestructibility as an athlete was fractured but I was determined to make a comeback.

My alcohol consumption decreased dramatically because I knew it would inhibit my physical healing process but my ignorant use of marijuana remained. Looking back I couldn't have been more foolish in that regard. I was undereducated on the harm that pot does and if this drug seems enticing to you I urge you to educate yourself. Use of this drug is nothing short of poisoning youself. Look it up.

I rehabilitated diligently and restructured my throwing motion and through this focused hard work I gained 10 miles per hour on my fast ball, making me a lefty that threw over 90mph. This put me back on the major league scout's radars and I was back on track in my mind as well. The "party animal" had re-emerged and I was once again feeling invincible.

After my senior season in college I got married, became a father of you, Tommy, and was drafted in the 6th round of the 1990 amateur draft by the Milwaukee Brewers. This reality change slowed my "party hardy" habits a bit. I loved my family very much but my Godless connection of drugs and alcohol to a good time still remained.

Upon signing my first professional contract I was then required to move thousands of miles away to start my minor league career. I remember becoming extremely focused on my career both mentally and physically and it paid off. I had a great beginning and was named "closest to the majors" in the entire Brewer organization in the highly respected publication, Baseball America. My baseball career was taking off and on top of that I got the great news that I was going to have another baby, this time a girl. Outside of being nearly broke, life couldn't have been any better, really. Then injuries and the travel began to take it's toll.

Unable to afford to bring my family along with me after my second season put untold stress on my family and relationships. The literal gap created between me and my family was difficult but in my mind we always had the off season to re-acquaint and patch things up. In the off-season of '93, (I think it was), I received an offer to play in a newly formed winter league in Arizona. All the top prospects were being invited and this would be a chance to showcase my abilities with the best. In my mind I would have been crazy to pass it up. It took all of ten minutes to make the decision to go.

Arizona was as beautiful as you would expect. The days were filled with perfect weather and talent filled baseball. The nights were equally as impressive. A party of rock star status could be found every night and I didn't maintain my off field focus. My selfishness and downright stupidity sent the season up in smoke and I went home with my tail between my legs, licking my wounds. But then came a chance to redeem myself, or so I thought.

The Venezuelan government had gone through a coup and one of the American major-league pitchers playing there decided he had had enough of the chaos and wanted to go home. I had a friend on the team that recommended me so I got the call just after I returned home in December. Despite legitimate objections from my wife, I went. I was okay with it because I was told I would be paid $3,000 for only a month of play....just a few more starts to get the team into the playoffs and then they would get someone else to fill my shoes. This is what I was told over the phone anyway.

At that time the Venezuelan league was second only to the American major leagues, so the exposure would be great. I could also earn three times the money I did during the minor league season in a third of the time which would enable me to take my wife and kids with me the next season. To me it was a no-brain-er.

Although I heard the sense of urgency in my wife's voice, and could clearly see the hurt in her eyes when she asked me to stay, beleiving that in the long run it would be what was best for us as a family, I reluctantly went anyway.

The organization I played for, The Caracas Leones, made it into the playoffs and because I had pitched well up to that point they "asked" me to stay for another month. My wife was counting on me coming home, and I planned to return as well, but then came the meetings. One with the players at the chapmionship celebration party and another with the owner. At the party I was fed enough rum and beer to inebriate an elephant but staved off the barrage of pleadings for me to stay. Although I was enjoying the new team and the players on it, I still felt my promise to my wife to be paramount. Then came the meeting with the owner. It was in that office that my naive eyes were opened to the business realities behind the game.

I was told that the $3,000 that I was promised over the phone would be paid in full to me *only* on the contingency that I fulfilled all requests of the organization and now they were *requesting* for me to stay for the playoffs. When I told them that this isn't how I understood the contract when it was explained to me over the phone I was ever so politely shown that it was all right there in the fine print, literally. The contract with my signature was unfolded in front of me and the writing being referred to was pointed out. I was then told that I could leave but they would only pay me $1,500, half of what I needed to take my family with me the next season. I had been officially baited and switched!

I remember the anger and sadness as if it were yesterday. I felt trapped and angry. In my mind my hands were tied and I sadly explained that over the phone to my wife back home. I did my best to convince her it was for the best, and hung up the phone. Then things went from bad to downright miserable.

The playoffs went horribly. The extra two weeks felt like a year. My pitching reflected my internal feelings of hollowness and my performances weere a shell of my ability. Our pitchers didn't pitch and our hitters didn't hit and and we were out of the playoffs within a week. Then, just when I thought it couldnt get any worse, I received yet another kick in the butt on the way out the door.

Strangely, on the day for us to leave and go home, I was the only American that didn't have a plane ticket waiting for me at the airport. When I was told that the next flight available wouldn't be until the next morning my heart hit my stomach and my stomach hit the floor! I literally wasn't sure that I was going to survive if I had to stay the night in the airport, and this was why.

My mind rushed back in time to the day of my arrival. I immediately recalled being warned by my pitching coach when we first met about the abundance of thieves and robberies, (as well as by the other American players, many times over), to a Venezuelan thief, an American passport was literally worth killing for. For this reason we had essentially two rules to live by. Keep your passport locked up in a safe place or in your possession at all times, and never travel alone. Even though I adhered to these rules as if my life depended on it, (which it did), I was still victimized on two separate occasions, the first of which occurred only days before while traveling to eat.

At that time in Caracas the only American fast food restaurants, McDonald's and Burger King, were located in the heart of the city so I, and four other players, would travel there via subway to have lunch from time to time. Going to these restaraunts was as close to being home as we could find. These were like holy temples to us, and to satisfy our ingrained need for American style food was seemingly worth risking our lives for. We had made this pilgrimage several times successfully so our confidence was high. However, on this particular run through chaos my innocence was lost.

After enjoying a small taste of the homeland we hopped back onto the subway just as we had done a handful of times before, only on this particular return home our grouping effort got twisted up and I was cleverly separated from the others.

While we were getting on the escalator that transported passengers up from the underbelly out to the street level, a man suddenly cut in front of me. He was just alittle guy so he didn't seem to pose a threat. And besides, my American friends were right in fron of him, so I simply kept my distance and rode my way up.

We ascended without incident until the very top of the

ride where he then suddenly dropped his subway ticket on the stairs at the top where the stairway disappeared under the concrete pad leading to the street. Suddenly the ticket was lifted into the air by the reversed air current created by the stairs continued motion under the landing and it began to levitate in front of him. It was like a magic trick!

The ticket was bobbing up and down like a butterfly and he was swatting at it and waking backwards at the same time! You see, the way the subway worked there at the time, (and probably still does), you needed to insert your ticket into a kiosk to open one of the many horizontally revolving bar gates at the top of the escalators to advance onto the street, so if you don't have a ticket, you can't get out.

Well, because I was immediately behind him I was then forced to suddenly take my hand out of my pocket, (and off my wallet), so I could balance myself while walking backwards in order to avoid running him over. I naturally bumped into the person behind me and this is when this man must have picked my wallet out of my front pocket. I say "must have" because besides the bumping into him I didn't feel a thing out of the ordinary and didn't even realize what had happened until several minutes later as I hurried to catch up with the others.

I recall feeling the relief of catching up to them but then the sudden hooror of my front pocket being empty. Realizing that I had been robbed I was both angry and scared. We all decided that chasing after the thief was pointless so we all cautiously headed back, looking forsard to the safety of our hotel rooms.

Couple this traumatic incident with the overall chaotic wild west lawlessness that ruled the land and yeah, if I were forced to stay the night in the airport, my life was definitely in danger.

With this memory still in the forefront of my mind I began frantically searching for the number of the Caracas Leones front office in everything that I had, beginning with my newly aquired wallet. After methodically peeling apart everything I had, I came to the stomach sickening realization that I didn't have it. I quickly calculated that my easiest way out of this increasingly dangererous situation would be to call my wife back in the states. I knew she had the number and could call the front office for me and have them send out what I envisioned at this point to be a rescue party.

With this less than reliable plan, I awkwardly lugged my giant suitcase in one hand and my little briefcase in the other around the dilapidated, third world airport.

I did my best to watch everyone around me with the voice of my pitching coach ringing in my ears, "some people here will kill ya for your passport so be on alert".

To get a phone line connection back to the United States I first had to find the phone booths of international lines, which were grouped together in one spot and located in the middle of everything. I hurriedly walked to the nearest open phone and picked it up, listening for an operator. The phone system there was, (and I'm sure still is), incredibly simplistic and straightforward. If you heard a busy signal when you put the phone to your ear then you had to hang up and try again.

After what seemed like an hour of trying to connect to the outside world I finally felt the relief of hearing someone in broken English ask me "which country?". Then my wife's voice on the other end was truly a HALLALUIA moment! Although relieved to hear her voice this most certainly didn't mean the potential for death and dimemberment was over. The challenge then became being heard and understood because the connection was so extremely faint. It was like trying to hear the smallest voice in the world while standing on a bustling concourse of a major league baseball game during the seventh inning stretch.

Then, just as I got through to my wife, I noticed a man pick up the phone in the open booth next to me. Knowing that I was going to have to literally yell, I turned away, putting my back to him in an attempt at politness. If I had known what he was about to do, being polite would have been the furthest thing from my mind! While explaining about the ticket mix up to my only life line out, this professional thief picked up my briefcase and probably calmly walked away. I had only taken my eyes off of it for a few moments and again like magic, POOF! It was gone!

I yelled at my wife to hold on and dropped the phone, letting it dangle by its cord. I hurriedly walked around to the other side of the phones to try to catch the thief. After quickly scanning the area there I then rushed back around to check on my last sole possession, my luggage full of my clothes and personal items. I was expecting to see someone running away with that too but thankfully it remained there on the floor next to the swaying phone receiver. Probably too heavy and bulky for a clean get away!

After internalizing the loss of my most valued possessions excluding my passport, I put the phone back up to my ear and angrily explained what had just happened to my wife. With the urgency of the situation hanging like a noose in the air, she made the call immediately. My *rescue team* turned out to be the same scatter toothed smiling guy that picked me up at the beginning of this whole fiasco. He was driving the same smelly, ready to break down, old, mostly American car, but I couldn't have been more relieved to climb in. I would have got on the back of a scooter at that point! I was back in my hotel room an hour later sipping a rum and coke to calm my nerves and proceeded to fly out the next day.

It probably goes without saying but I have been extremely hesitant to travel outside the United States ever since.

As far as the next year was concerned, there was no change in the downward spiral of the one before.

First my Dad passed away from cancer of the brain, then I suffered a season ending injury of a broken facial bone and crushed sinus from being hit in the right eye with a line drive during batting practice that I didn't even throw! And if that wasn't enough to make me turn to God, the next thing should have been!

Two weeks into spring training my wife called and told me that she wanted a divorce! Although I recall being quite literally knocked down to my knees, my pride still wouldn't allow me to pray for God's assistance and I still didn't think He was anything but a fable.

In retrospect I see now that my self-pride was so large and in charge that I simply didn't have room for God. I only recall feeling my desire for excelling as a professional baseball pitcher change from a passion into an obsession. I actually recall telling myself that I was "now married to baseball" and there was nothing short of career ending injury that would keep me from getting to the Major leagues. My life's existence was centered around working my tail off to get better at the craft of pitching during the day and partying my tail off at night to numb the pain of not being able to see or talk to my children.

I suffered many ups and downs throughout the

remainder of my career and I never acheived the goal of the millions of dollars that I once felt destined to receive. I look back now and wholeheartedly thank God that I didn't achieve millionaire status because I know now that with my attitude of invincibility backed by a seemingly endless flow of cash at the big league level, I would have only partied my way into rehab. I was so twisted and broken on the inside that I didn't have the self-discipline off the field to do the right thing, and I now realize that of course God knew that as well. Although I was oblivious to it at the time, God wasn't taking anyuthing away from me, He was protecting me from myself.

I disappointingly retired from baseball in 1998 but my inward looking, self serving ways continued....that is until the "Arizona enlightenment".

3

THE VEIL IS TORN!

It was just before dawn on the fourth morning of another restless and irritating night. I'd been rolling around on the sofa wide awake from about 4:30am on, trying every position available to me but just couldn't get back to sleep. Once again, I got up just before dawn. I brewed up a cup of breakfast blend coffee and then crept quietly out to the sun deck to catch the Arizona sunrise. This 8' x 16' man made oasis was where I would routinely regain my positive perspective each morning.

The scenery from this deck is mundane. It's comprised primarily of desert with pieces of civilization dropped in here and there with a highway cut through it.

Stretching to the left I could see the beginning of the city of Yuma. To the right, in the distance there were jagged hillsides of rock rising and falling away from me. The deck was elevated which allowed me to barely look over a 5 ft., cream colored, cinder block wall. The view was certainly not one of pure and uncluttered nature. To the direct left of the deck was a small, 30' x 10' toolshed/shop. Looking beyond that I could see the butt end of a row of ten or so similar lots with mini houses and motor homes that sloped gently down toward the main street that exited the mostly snowbird community.

Immediately to the right, beyond the walled backyard there was one more house that showed only its rooftop. This was essentially the end of our street as the road turned to the right as it continued through the neighborhood. These neighbors have a medium sized desert tree rising above their side of the wall that adds some beauty but nothing to write home about.

Directly ahead of the wall in front of the deck I was sitting on is an open slice of desert that stretches forward about two hundred yards and is approximately three hundred yards wide. Nothing appears to be alive in this barren strip of sand filled landscape except maybe an unseen lizard or two, but there is a smattering of sage bushes with an occasional piece of windblown debris clinging to it here and there, which gives only the appearance of life.

Beyond all this there is a surprisingly busy highway running parallel to where I sit. I say surprisingly busy because it felt like I was truly in the middle of nowhere, yet humanity was all around me somehow finding a way to live here.

A train travels through the sagebrush infested

land out beyond the highway blowing it's whistle now and then, which adds to the *flavor* of the morning. Having eyed this scenery for three consecutive days, I found myself averting my gaze to the sky on this particular morning as I tried to achieve a more positive perspective.

The sky was a painting of low flying, large white billowing clouds mixed with even lower hanging, wispy but giant vapors. Incredibly, the clouds were floating both east and west at the same time, traveling over and under one another and sometimes colliding making them intriguing to watch. The desert sky that morning was definitely presenting a "heavenly" ballet. I reclined in the "easy chair styled" lawn chair and began to take in the show. Reflecting back now I believe that it was at this time when it ALL began. I still can't pinpoint it but this natural occurrence was both awesome and supernatural and stands out like an absolute miracle to this day.

As I gazed upward everything suddenly took on a deeper and newer three dimensional beauty. The clouds became more vivid. I could now see every plume clearly in great detail as they hovered above. Then, suddenly, the clouds seemed to take on a life of their own and began expanding and contracting, as if they were now breathing.

I also noticed that the once flat, light blue high sky backdrop was suddenly transformed into something much deeper and much more dynamic. It was as if a whole new dimension was suddenly added and I could now see that the sky was actually millions and millions of miles deep and incredibly vibrant. The heavens suddenly became an intensely beautiful ocean of multidimensional artwork, the likes of which I had never seen before.

I was transfixed and couldn't turn away.

I remember saying to myself out loud, "even the greatest of man's artistic creations pale in comparison to the art of God."

Even though it was an incredibly spiritual moment, I didn't recognize that at the time. I only recall feeling all of my anger and grumpiness melting away, replaced with a warm love that flooded my entire body from the inside out.

I felt so amazed at this that I'm positive an open mouthed smile of joy covered my face. I felt dumbfounded and awestruck at the same time. It felt as if I was witnessing a true miracle.

I then remember simply relaxing and taking in the show for what I figure must have been 20 minutes or so. Enough time to let my coffee go cold anyway.

It was truly an awakening to a love that I had never felt so deeply before. I still struggle to find the words to describe it. I mean, how can words relay a miracle?

Since this experience I've been trying to make sense of it. I've even thought that maybe everyone else already sees the sky this way, and that maybe I'm the oddball, but I tell you, it wasn't until that morning that my eyes were opened to this three dimensionally created sky. Looking back, I now believe that this was the exact time my eyes and ears and heart were opened to God. In that 15 to 20 minute span of time I was completely immersed in great and true love. It was so incredible that I forgot about my wonderful cup of coffee. When I lifted my cup of coffee to my lips I realized it had gone cold. I reluctantly got up to go back inside to warm it up and that's when things got irritatingly normal again.

Halfway back to the front door the crankiness

started creeping back in, I remember I stopped in my tracks. I shut my eyes and paused my body and my mind and I took my mind back to the wonder that I had just witnessed and the love that I felt in those moments and suddenly my perspective came back to joyful bliss, pushing the negativity away. This was both new and awesome and I realized that I was able to raise a feeling of calmness quite easily. Still somewhat stunned, I resumed my walk to the kitchen smiling, filled once more with love.

This newly found ability to instantly change my perspective for the better was in itself intriguing, but I did not suspect that God was working on me directly. Simply put, I wasn't looking for His help, I was just trying to enjoy a cup of coffee. My perspective of my life at that time was just fine. In fact, I had actually felt like I was still somewhat on top of my game. As far as I was concerned, the only thing in my life that was negative was the bad sleep I was getting. I felt very conscious of, and extremely thankful for, all that I had. I fully recognized that my immediate family was, (and is), an awesome gift given to me as a second chance at my dream life that I had lost in my divorce. It had always been my half-hearted feeling that God had led me down this path. I wasn't looking for guidance or help, and yet it came. This is still baffling to me.

I'd heard of this sort of change happening to people during a time of deep despair but I really wasn't in despair. And besides, I have never really been "spiritual" enough to seek out an experience like that in the first place. For The Holy Spirit to elevate one's life seemed to me at the time to be something that others made up. To put it bluntly, I just didn't think it was true.

In my mind I was a very lucky person and I wasn't looking for help of ANY kind from ANYONE, and yet this and many other unsolicited, incredibly profound changes were about to take place in my life.

God wasn't about to just come into my life, he was about to announce his presence with authority!

4

BACK TO "REALITY"

After re-heating my coffee I headed back out to sit on the sundeck for some more "perspective therapy". The totally enlightened feeling of love was still glowing within me. I was loving all things as well as seeing love emitting from everything visible. This is when I think that God really hit me with both barrels, but still not reading the clues, I didn't know it. As I think back it was at that moment that I was enlightened to a fresh new understanding of real love and it's true depth, but because I wasn't trying to attain anything but a positive perspective, I didn't know it was God.

Another part of my past spiritual growth that should be revealed is the fact that for the 10 years prior to the experience in the desert I clung to the idea of love being everywhere, and flowing from all that is natural all the time. I'd tried consistently to work on this positive perspective. To have peace in my heart and mind has always been a goal of mine, but it wasn't until that very moment that I stopped just looking and hoping for it and started to actually SEE and really FEEL it with consistency. It was as if a shaded veil had been lifted from my eyes allowing me to see the world on a new love-filled level. This may sound like a cliche but it is what I really felt! I had never felt so much love all at once. It was like being immersed in a warm, thick velvety fluid of love and deep, deep joy. I really can't totally put into words what I was feeling, but I can say that it was absolutely soul deep.

Soon after this my wife Heidi came out and joined me. I wanted so badly to share this new found awesome magnificence with her, but I couldn't put together any combination of words to explain it properly. Still fully immersed in the moment, the best my sensory overloaded mind could come up with was to clumsily point out how I thought the sky and clouds looked exceptionally strange and beautiful. Looking back she must have thought I was nuts.

Being the sweetheart-ed person that she is she tried to see what I was carryin' on about. She looked up at them in curiosity, but not much else was said about it. We chatted a bit and life went on as usual.

The intensity of the feeling slowly dulled with the exchange of thoughts and plans for the upcoming day. The only residual effect was the ability to summon that same inner peace and love to my heart almost immediately in any time of turbulence by recalling the wonder in the sky that day. Other than that everything returned to "normal."

Although profoundly changed that day, I am still always being reminded that I am nothing more than a flawed human. I still feel anger when it approaches and sometimes I momentarily lose perspective. Heidi and I still have minor disagreements where voices get elevated. I still experience times of angry impatience with my children when the irrational and craziness that surfaces in the course of parenting rears its unexpected head. But after the Yuma encounter I am able to regain my love-filled perspective much more quickly, (and here's the key), without holding a grudge. In fact it was an experience of just such craziness with my son one afternoon that showed me just how real this is, but that occurrence I will explain later. First I think it's important to create a road map of the changes upon returning home in a more detailed way. My hope is that this will help me better understand what is involuntarily happening to me.

5

CURIOSITY OVERLOAD

On the first night after we got back from vacation I was flipping through our recordings on the DVR and saw that I had recorded 'The Bible' series on the History channel. I'd recorded the entire series some time ago for basically two reasons. One being to sit and watch it with my wife on those Sunday evenings that we didn't make it to church.

Ya see, at that time in my life going to church was little more than an inconvenience that I tolerated for the sake of your spiritual growth. After all, I was an avid fantasy football addict and in that world there were just some games that couldn't be missed.

My other reason for taping it was that I could take the easy path to avoid actually reading the Bible. I had made an attempt at reading the Bible at a younger time in my life but just couldn't wrap my brain around it past the first few pages of Genesis. It just didn't speak to me at that time of my life and the unfamiliar wording kept getting in the way, so I gave in. This History channel series, I felt was the perfect solution but I just never seemed to have time to follow up.

So there I was, sitting on our couch comfortably DVR surfing for something to watch and nearly flipped past it once again. But, on this particular night, something stopped me and I guess that's when things began to stir. I wasn't looking to become a more spiritual person, I just thought, why not? And so I watched.

I recall watching the first part of the series, Genesis. I didn't get through the whole episode, it got late and I shut it off just after Abraham rescued Lot. It didn't make any more of an impact than any other movie ever had. I just remember thinking that it was worth checking out at another time and then went to bed. The next morning is when my obsession began.

Looking back now, I don't recall the time or day that my pursuit of Jesus actually began, I only remember that the more I learned about His life, the more my curiosity grew.

I don't know if the fact that it was the week leading up to the Easter holiday had anything to do with what was about to occur in my life, but it was indeed that week. In the past, Easter always came and went and the only thing I ever really looked for were eggs and candy, (and occasionally an egg with money in it, depending on the party style I was attending), but this year something brought about a change in me and it was VERY different to say the least! In fact, before this year I hadn't even fully considered just how deeply important Easter is for a Christian. It's not that I didn't understand that this is the day that we celebrate Jesus overcoming the grave, it's that I never before gave it it's due gravity. A curiosity that had seemingly come from nowhere didn't just begin to grow within me, it began taking me over.

At that point in time I still hadn't drawn a correlation between what was going on within me and the experience that I'd had on the sun deck in Yuma the week prior. Actually, I still hadn't even given it a second thought. All I knew was that I needed to learn more about the life of Jesus, plain and simple. I began to watch and read everything I could get my hands and eyes on about the life and times of Jesus Christ. I even watched the Mel Gibson movie 'THE PASSION OF THE CHRIST', which I thought I would never do because of the brutality that I'd heard it portrayed. I'd heard that it was an excellent movie, but that the flogging scene in particular was quite savage and I'm just NOT a fan of watching violence in any way shape or form but for some strange reason, I now felt compelled to watch.

I actually remember at one point during the dark and brutal flogging scene I caught myself looking away and then having to refocus, I was quite literally forcing myself to watch. I actually remember saying out loud to myself "to watch it is the absolute least I can do after what he did for me" so in painful horror, I watched.

Through cringing eyes I absorbed it, and now, strangely, I'm so thankful I did. Thankful because it was in watching that scene of torture that I fully realized just what it was that Jesus knowingly and willfully endured for me. I realize that there's no way that we can truly know exactly what it was that He endured before his death but I bet this was pretty close. Reflecting on it now I realize that it was then that an intensity of my love for Him began to take on a life of it's own. I had suddenly felt a love for my Savior that I'd never felt before. The statement "Jesus died for our sins" took on a whole new meaning for me. Also, in looking back now I see that this newly-found feeling of love and respect also fueled my fire for the knowledge of not just his walk, but The Bible in it's entirety.

I knew the knowledge that I was suddenly craving could only be found within the actual Bible so my quest to read it from cover to cover began right then and there. I wanted to know my Father's heart from that point forward. I would also advise anyone, believer and unbeliever alike, to read and interpret this masterful book for yourself. After all, no one worth their salt would pass judgment on anything without first completely educating one's self on the subject first, would he/she?

Looking back on it now, the closest I can come to pinpointing the beginning of my being "born again" was at that moment when I was watching Jesus being scourged. I think it was somewhere within those split seconds that I fully accepted the existence of God and at the same time fell in love with Him. I recall suddenly having no doubt in my mind.

This enlightenment permeated my heart as well. I came away from that movie dramatically changed. I don't know how it could be that all doubt could suddenly be gone just from seeing that scene, but it was. Without a shred of doubt the certainty of God's existence and my love for Him had taken over my heart and soul. What also continues to amaze me is the absoluteness of it all. I can't even summon up the smallest fiber of doubt about Father God in any way shape or form anymore. It's as if I knew it all along, but I know that I didn't. The reality of His existence has become instinctively true to me. Our Creator had inserted into my heart the miracle of proof and I DIDN'T ask for it. Even though I hadn't seen a miracle like the parting of the Red sea with my eyes, I had felt one of the same magnitude with my heart and mind and now I see His miracles all around me all the time.

As for the profound physical changes, this is

where it really took an unexpected twist!

6

THE CHANGES BEGIN

Oddly, the first and most concrete physical change I recognized was that everything tasted better--- much better. Along with my emotional sensitivity being raised, (tears formed at nearly everything), so too have my external senses. Now when I eat, the flavors and textures are much more intense. Food that was once good now tastes like one of the best things I've ever eaten! This has been an incredible surprise but, just as everything can be both a blessing and a curse, so can this. I know by the looks I get from my wife that it becomes tiresome to hear me continually rave about how awesome my Cheerios taste. Toning this down so as not to be annoying was a bit of a challenge at first because I so wanted everyone to know how great I was feeling, hoping that it would somehow make them feel great as well, I guess. But, what was once an incredible, supernatural difference has become my new normal so that has changed as well.

I have also found that my taste in music has dramatically changed, I used to listen primarily to country and/or all genres of rock, and now it's rare that I have anything on or in my head besides contemporary Christian rock. This is definitely strange! Before, my ego would never allow me to listen to this style of music because I felt that I was strong and Christian rock was only for the weak people that needed uplifting. I thought the music was uplifting and happy, but I held the view that it was created for those who were having trouble in their lives. Although pleasing to the ears and uplifting, it just wasn't appealing to me because I was happy, and seeking nothing in my life. Now I hear the lyrics and it ALL pertains to me in one way or another. I know now that before I could hear it but I wasn't able to understand what was being said and relayed in the lyrics. Now, I not only hear it, but the lyrics speak specifically to me. It is both scary and enlightening.

For instance, being "set free" is a common phrase in Christian rock. Before my veil lifting this was a phrase that carried no meaning to me because I didn't realize that I was a slave. A slave to the sins of the flesh, drugs and alcohol, fears of all kinds. When adversity struck these compulsions cried "come to me!" and I would run to only be momentarily pacified and then let down once again. Now that I have been set free through my redemption, I get it. Now, when I hear about being set free I realize that they are about the lifting of the veil which gives me the ability to see beyond the false reality that we trap ourselves in daily. Being set free is about not being a slave to the temporary void fillers and instead being full all of the time with His love! Understanding this is truly as freeing an experience as a person can feel and it is absolutely exhilarating!

Equally astounding to me is this sudden discerning that came not from learning due to reading or hearing information.....it came from within. I didn't have someone explain it to me or read it and then suddenly say to myself 'oh, now I get it', no, I all of a sudden just got it! Which is a far cry from not even wanting to listen to this musical style.

Another amazing thing to me is that this implanted knowledge and true wisdom also sets me free of all internal struggle and fears, and, this newly created void has been filled with the pure love of our Father in heaven.

WOW what a feeling!!

I'm not boasting when I say it just doesn't get any better, I merely want to proclaim it to the world to give those that are like I was before my liberation hope. Hope in knowing that if God is real and willing to give a wretch like me His amazing grace so with your absolute belief He will certainly give to you as well.

I used to hear the song Amazing Grace and thought that it was only a song played at funerals. Now I know differently because it speaks directly to me as one who has truly received His unconditional love. I used to think that His love came only on the condition that I had to be at least trying to walk righteously in a consistent manner but because He came to me under no conditions whatsoever, I now KNOW differently.

I wasn't sad and looking for Him. I wasn't happy and looking for Him. I WASN'T LOOKING FOR HIM AT ALL! If His love were conditional why would He come to me? This makes me want to be a servant to God.

Before, I thought the lyrics about "chains being broken" was a metaphor for dying and one's spirit then ascending to heaven. I understand now the true meaning is experiencing the freedom from the slavery that comes with sin.

I know in my heart that I will be in heaven one day because I know I am His. I am a child of God. Given this fact, what is there to fear? I continue to be mystified by this profound liberation that came out of the blue. "I've been set free" couldn't ring more true for me. But again, I can't help but ask myself, why me and why now?

A "door for Jesus to walk through" are the words from another awesome gospel song. I can now completely relate to that musical phrase because that is exactly what I aspire to be, a door for Jesus at all times, not just when I walk through the doors of where I worship.

My spirituality used to be something I could put on and take off, but not anymore because the Spirit just won't allow it. My thoughts are on God in some way nearly 100% now. I say nearly because to say otherwise would be false. I do deal with the world from time to time so in doing so I take my mind off Him but outside of that I have a hunger for Him and His word that just won't quit.

Another major change involved alcohol. Before this transformation I would have at least one drink every night and sometimes a few too many. Now I abstain completely. It wasn't overnight but I have willingly turned completely away without help from anyone but God. It's not that I see getting drunk as something that everyone shouldn't do, I mean come on, who am I to judge? It's just something that I shouldn't do, which is laughable considering my prior attitude of being a macho male.

The old me would scoff at the new me and teasingly call him a quitter and other belittling names, that's just how I was. The fact is I have changed and am no longer that person. I feel that person inside of me slowly dying and I couldn't feel better. Alcohol doesn't hold the appeal it once did because it masks out the feeling of His love that now fills my soul.

The idea of being drunk is now completely undesirable to me, even when I'm in a party situation. I no longer have the urge to get "hammered" or even dulling my senses in the slightest. In fact, I now relish my sobriety because I see and feel life in a completely different, and wonderful way. It's like I am already 'high' with a happiness that dwarfs the man-made high of drugs and alcohol. In fact, getting inebriated is a buzz kill now!

I also realize that I now feel something that I haven't felt for a long, long time---- a healthy attitude toward life that I didn't even realize I was missing because it was so masked. I know now that I was self absorbed about life and THAT lifestyle in and of itself was extremely unhealthy.

My wants and desires have now completely changed and all of this occurred without any one person telling me that I should change, including myself! Again, the change came from within me, and to me the unearthly part continues to be, I didn't even try to consciously make the change, IT JUST HAPPENED!

As unbelievable as this may sound, I know that this change is real because I can physically feel it inhabiting my body. This is just one more pruning that has taken place as a part of my transformation I guess.

Another pronounced change from my previous lifestyle is that I get up earlier,... much earlier. When I say earlier, I'm talking between 4:30 and 5am, and I am excited to do so. I have found this to be the the most peaceful part of the day to exercise my new, seemingly injected passion, which is to study of The Bible and meditate on it.

I now see everything in the world around me differently. Before this experience I saw and judged people on their surface appearance. I thought their faces portrayed them,---- happy, sad, mean, outgoing, etc. but that was as deep as I would look. I now realize that underneath that superficial impression based on outward emotional appearance we are all actually the same, we are all children of God. Sure, these emotions are still present but my instantly biased feeling toward people according to their facial expression has vanished. I now first feel love for everyone.

Where there once was judgment, fear and hesitation there is now love, compassion and understanding. I cannot relay in words how awesome this single change of outlook has made in my life. If only I could give just this one wholeheartedly beautiful perspective to others in a everlasting pill, it would truly change the world. I now find myself constantly asking the question, why is it so hard for people to just love one another? I now know that it's the veil. The veil of the false reality keeps us all apart from His love and it is so deeply sad to me now.

I've also found that my new found peace also gives me patience like I never had before. I have always considered myself a patient person, but in stark comparison to now, I had the patience of a 10 year old. This particular change didn't take place overnight either, but it has taken place with very little effort. I still struggle at times to keep a Good first perspective but it doesn't take long to adjust it back.

Another major difference is my old self was always

on a much tighter schedule, but now I can see that this is a false reality as well. Before I would get upset at anything that would alter my mental itinerary, regardless of who or what it was. Not that I would throw a fit or even raise my voice, I would actually internalize it. I would hold it in and let it fester until something severe enough to pop the cork would come along and it was then that I would vent by raising my voice and cursing like an uneducated child. But now I truly understand that patience really is a virtue and exercising that wisdom allows Jesus to walk through me. Even as I am writing this my heart is overflowing with the joyful comfort of feeling this miracle that has been bestowed upon me. Both my heart and mind have gone through a profound transition. Fear has been replaced with love and patience; anger with passiveness and understanding. I think this profound virtue may be as great a gift as can be accepted from God. The "accepting" I speak of I learned by what happened next with you my children, which shook me to the absolute   core.

7

FORSAKEN?

It was one day shy of a month exactly since the "sun deck awakening". I awoke the same way I had over the past month, thinking about God and filled with his love. God and Jesus had become what woke me and put me to sleep every day.

It was Sunday and I was taking a shower, getting ready for the day while listening to my new 'must have' Christian music when the phone rang. Figuring I only had a few more minutes before I would be finished, I let it go to voice mail. After getting dried off I checked the message and surprisingly it was from some friends that I had invited to go to church with us a few weeks prior. They were calling to say that they would meet us there and I was very happy to hear they wanted to go. I finished getting ready and went downstairs to tell my wife the good news and soon thereafter we were on our way to church. We arrived there in the usual kind of way and the service was one of the best that I had been to so I was excited at the prospect of my friends enjoying it enough to come back. We shook hands with the Pastor and introduced him to our friends and then started on our way home and this is when it happened.

Services end at noon and we were only a few minutes from church, so I figure it was about 12:15 when I suddenly realized that I'd completely lost the spiritual enlightenment. The feeling of joy was gone, but it was more than that. I recall feeling like my 'old self' in an instant and wondering what was going on with me. It was as if a callous had covered my heart. I became quick tempered again and the heaven sent elation and joy were completely gone without a trace. I literally felt like nothing profound had ever happened to me.

I was confused and unable to fully grasp it, (in fact I still don't know if I really grasp it even now). I began to think that I must have done something to displease God so I began frantically to search through the past 24 hours in an attempt to pinpoint what may have triggered this about-face.

The only thing different in my life that I could come up with was the fact that I had fasted the day before. I did this because I had been studying the old testament and had read how people had fasted as a way to become closer to God. And, during that experience I felt like the Lord was with me because I was not hungry during the entire time. I wondered, could that have caused the backsliding? I doubted it so I kept replaying the past hours and ultimately decided to let it be until morning. I prayed to be forgiven and went to bed depressed, hoping for God's repossession.

The next day came and the feeling of absolute love for everyone and everything was still completely absent. It wasn't like I hated everyone, it's just that the happiness that had previously flooded my heart just wasn't there. My senses were duller and I remember feeling like I was now merely "going through the motions" of daily life. Another big tell was that the Christian gospel music had suddenly lost its appeal. EVERYTHING had reverted. I was literally feeling rotten inside. I was so disturbed by lunchtime that I nearly e-mailed my wife at work to tell finally her, but again held off. I figured as a public school teacher she has enough stress to deal with, let alone my weird stuff. Then something shocking happened around 12:30 pm that once again changed everything.

My four-year old son Colby and I were playing a game I call cars when he suddenly, without any warning had a complete melt down that caught me entirely off guard. Apparently I had done something that didn't meet his expectations so he reacted by verbally erupting at me, yelling at the top of his little lungs. He screamed that I wasn't playing the way he wanted me to and slammed his Hot Wheel to the floor and then fell to his knees crying uncontrollably. In my initial shock and confusion I remember feeling instant anger and wanting to yell back at him but, astonishingly, my mind paused. I stood there looking at him kneeling, crying with his head bowed and hands covering his face. Then I instantly recalled the day earlier. I was taken back to a moment when my daughter had a similar melt down with my wife.

We were getting ready to go to church

services when she and my daughter had a seemingly minor disagreement that somehow erupted into Mt. St. Helen's, 1980. My wise and experienced wife had had enough and rather than continue the power struggle she intelligently walked away from it and asked me to deal with it. I remembered looking at my beyond upset daughter and thinking to myself, 'what would Jesus do?' I then knelt down and took her into my arms and told her that I understood and that everything would be alright. I repeated this a few more times and she settled down so that we could continue getting ready to go. This was almost exactly the same situation so, again, a voice in my head told me to go to Colby in the same way. I did. I remember kneeling down and scooping my son into my arms and while sitting together on the floor I repeated those same calming words, "it's okay, I understand" over and over again. After Colby had calmed down the 'feeling' of peace and joy returned in me. All of a sudden I felt the warmth fill me again and the callous on my heart melted away. I wept with happiness right there with my son on my lap, both of us enveloped with the thick blanket of Jesus wrapped around us. It was as if Jesus Himself knelt down and hugged us both right then and there.

Every day since, my heart has been filled with joy and what I know is the love of God. This isn't to say there hasn't been bumps in the road since then because there has. I wasn't suddenly transformed into a Saint that afternoon, but at least now, He has come back to live in me once again.

Why He left, I can only speculate. I have asked this question and been led to discern only that I have been strengthened. But strengthened for what?

8

TAKING THE BACK SEAT

Immediately after watching all of the movies I could find on the life of Jesus Christ my undivided attention shifted to the word of God and my study of the Bible began. It was as if I couldn't take it in fast enough. To say that I am driven is an untrue statement because I don't feel that I am entirely in control. It's more like I am being driven. What began as curiosity has grown to obsession. The old me would take one look at what my life consists of today and conclude insanity.

I asked my wife one night while lying in bed if she thought what was happening to me was strange and I will never forget what she said. Her words opened my mind up to understand just how strange it must be from the outside looking in. She said, "well Tom it's like this. If I were to take up knitting and then ALL I did from the time I rose in the morning to the time I went to bed was knit, that's what you are like now". Now I get it, but what do I do about it?

Outside of being a father and husband, worship in some form has all but consumed my life. This is dramatically different from the partying attitude that once dominated me.

Furthermore, my overall perspective on life's occurrences has completely changed. I now starkly see and hear in all directions a false reality based on our pursuit of inward looking, personally satisfying goals instead of concerning ourselves with what Our Father actually wishes us to be which is consistently selfless and loving toward Him and each other, just as Jesus told us to be.

This previous focus, (or arguably lack of focus), has distracted me in the past and continues to distract the vast majority of us from the real truth, more commonly called the "secret" to life. Having been eyes wide open for over a year now I've come to know the "secret" this way. We must fully internalize that God's will is being worked out all around you at ALL times. This also means we must conclude that the amount of control that we actually have is relegated to choosing between listening to His quiet voice or not. Put more simply, using our God given free will in the right way ALL of the time, not just when we feel like we are getting out of balance.

The sticky part to me is this. I know I couldn't have done this without The Creator's help so how can I expect anyone else to be able to do this by merely reading these words? And so I pray. I pray everyday for the Spirit to be poured out on all mankind just as it has been on me for I also know that if it isn't then mankind will ultimately destroy this miraculous creation that our father has left us in charge of.

I've also succumbed to the fact that no one can truly know God's will because then it becomes our will. We can, however, know and fully internalize that whatever happens is indeed His will and accept it as such. Unfortunately the difficulty in keeping this perspective begins almost immediately, but why? Why can't we stay in touch? I believe it to be self pride. We love to believe that we are in charge, that we have control over our destinies. After all, isn't it you that solved the problem at work or created the loving environment at home for your family? Aren't you the one that helped that child become what he or she is today, (given that they turned out good, right)? Our pride says wholeheartedly, YES! But, the reality is that it was God. Then, into the thought process creeps the idea that God wouldn't do unloving things to His children, so everything isn't His will, right? To that I say, correct, some of it is your will, and that's when we get into trouble.

This is when it gets tricky because it now comes down to faith. Our faith, or lack thereof, determines just how true this statement is for you individually. How much do you really trust God?

What I know to be true for me is that I now see God in everything, everywhere so it is easy for me to also see that He is in control of everything in and around my life, which is because I let Him be.

I seek to do His will and be His servant in everything I do, and so therefore I do His will and I am His servant. And so I ask, do you give Him this much control of your life? I suggest you at least try it and see the difference for yourself. The key though is this. It must be done wholeheartedly and filled with faith in God, not as a test to see if He is real.

With this sudden gift of complete and wholehearted faith I feel like I would be stupid not to. When a slave is set free would it be right to tell the master no, I want to remain a slave? This is how I feel having been set free from the bondage of the sins that once ruled over me.

Ponder this. Moses, in Deuteronomy and then Jesus in the books of Luke, Matthew and Mark tell us of the greatest commandment, that we should 'love God with all our hearts, mind and strength.'1 Was this not God speaking through Moses and Jesus telling us His/God's wishes?

Even for the less then faith-filled it is easy to comprehend that God was speaking.

Why then is it hard to believe that our Father in heaven doesn't use this same method to communicate to His children today as well? Is He a different God now than He was back then? Of course not. God hasn't changed, but our perception of God has.

And so I ask this again, how much faith do you have?

Are you giving Him control? Are you putting Him first all of the time in all situations?

I don't ask this to point out my strengths and your weaknesses my child, I ask this to give you the proper perspective so you can be His and feel His beautiful love just as I do. And I know this, because we are told in Matthew 6:33 that if we put Him first all these things, (food, clothing our most basic needs and then some!), will be given to us we must put Him first.

With the freely given gift of His Helper this is easy for me now whereas I know I couldn't have done it before, no matter how hard I tried and this is what concerns me for you because I want you to have it too, I just don't know how I can give it to you other than telling you of my experience.

I now realize that because I am one of His elect that our Father in heaven was in control then, and continues to be now. And with my submission His love continues to fill my heart to this day. A feeling of love that I can only relate to others as the same incredible feeling that you may have experienced when you felt the love of your first love, only better!

My prayer for you my sweethearts is that you have it too, that's all.

1   Deuteronomy 6:4, Matthew 22:37, Mark 12:30-31, Luke 10:27

9

CONTENT TO DANCE AND MOURN

Well sweetheart, things have quieted down in my soul. I now feel a balance in my life that wasn't there before. This is incredibly comforting. My question 'why me' is still a mystery and I will continue to search for the answer. It could be that I am one of His beloved or an answer to a previous prayer that I've somehow forgotten about? It remains baffling to me how this all started and how the pursuit of God's will has filled my every moment in life up to this point. I can't help but wonder if my obsession with the study of the Bible is a preparation for something.

It confounds me because I've been trained since I was old enough to do chores around the farm that "what we get is what we earn". So, the fact that

I received this miraculous gift of grace for absolutely nothing upsets my learned natural order of how the world works.

Sociologically speaking, learning the value of a buck is extremely important in this culture and I so am training my children the very same way, but I can't help but wonder if I'm doing the right thing.

This training, I think, is why it's so perplexing to me and unbelievable to those I try to talk about it with. And, although the importance of "learning to earn" is indisputably important among the wise, getting something for nothing has become the American dream. Isn't the goal to become wealthy without having to work? As someone that hired and fired workers in my landscaping business it sure seemed like it! To get someone that wanted to actually work hard for the money they were earning was only a dream for me.

This fact gives further evidence to just how far we've strayed as a nation.

And so in my case God gave His grace to me for FREE but yet when I tell of this to others I feel they have no choice but to refuse to believe it. I can't help but question why.

It reminds me of the scripture, "I played the pipe for you, you did not dance, I played a dirge for you, you did not mourn."Matthew 11:17

In breaking it down I know in my heart what our Father wants for all of His children is to enjoy this life that He gave us in a way that is pleasing to Him, and this I now can't help but do. I'm going to enjoy each moment God has given me as his servant, knowing that everything I do is for Him and because of Him.

As for what is happening and why, only time will tell but until then I will dance and I will mourn.

10

NEVER ALONE

It is now October 6th, 2014 my child and it was mid-April that my life took on new meaning through, what I have come to realize by reading the scriptures, is the filling of my heart and soul with the Holy Spirit.

This road, which has been a gift from God, has been truly miraculous. Yet as awesome and magical as it has been, it has also felt like somewhat of a curse at times. I say this because since being led to and having fallen in love with Jesus I have felt both blessed and confused and also a bit lonely.

One would think the blessing of fearlessness would be enough to overshadow any negativity. I mean how great is it to have ALL doubt removed from your heart about God? With this knowledge, seemingly injected into my heart came the removal of all fear, and the knowledge of this is true and real. Knowing this, how can anything negative come even close to one's heart? Yet things still do.

Puzzlement comes from the ever present question of why me and why now? Questions that only He can answer. So, my initial reaction was that maybe He was preparing me for something. Could it be my own death, or even worse, the death of someone close to me? Could it be that I am being shown the way for the sake of you, my children, or someone that I have yet to meet? These questions nearly overwhelmed me at first so I began to search the Bible for answers as I read it from cover to cover. Then the book of Joel, (specifically chapter 2), came along and the end times became my focus.

In this passage it is prophesied that in the end times "God will pour out His spirit on all His people." and this is to happen just before "the coming of the great and dreadful day of the Lord." so my eyes became fixed on the sky.

I began to see everything as a sign that the end was coming soon. I tried to talk about it with everyone from my best friend to my pastor and they all of course reassured me that my worry was unwarranted, so I backed off.

Through God's guidance these questions have become less and less important. I've come to the realization that having been given the gift of unwavering faith IS THE GIFT. THIS should be understood and embraced because, beyond that, nothing else really matters. The answer as to why has become less and less important as the days go by. And yet the loneliness still persists.

The loneliness comes from not being able to talk to anyone that has had this same life changing experience. It comes from not being sure who will understand and who will reject. Of course I know that He is always with me and there to talk to, (boy do I know that!), but to be able to hear someone else speak to me that has had a similar experience would allow me to confirm what I am feeling. Perhaps I'd feel a little less crazy. And I'm sure that when I am off the milk and onto solid food God will show me that path as well. So, I will remain patient and wholeheartedly grateful for just being chosen by God for whatever it is that He has in store for me for I am truly a humble servant and happy to be that. I have however, been guided to some new understandings since this has all occurred and the main one is about Love.

11

WHAT IS LOVE?

I now realize the love I previously knew was
self indulgent. In fact I, like many in this culture,
thought that love for one's self was of utmost
importance, not just for me, but also for the health of
those around me. I subscribed to the train of thought
that if I wasn't happy then the aura from that would
make those around me unhappy as well? I now
know that I was right in one sense but in another I
couldn't have been more wrong.

It's true that one's internal happiness is cast
upon those within immediate touch but upon being

72

filled with the Holy Spirit, now ALL of my love has been slowly changing to project outward, and in turn I have never felt more personally loved in my whole life. This love for the world creates happiness in me that before I had no idea was possible. I have always found great pleasure in seeing happiness brought to others, but this is happening at a whole different level.

I recall wondering how Mother Mary and people like her could do what they do and find true self fulfillment. I thought, 'how can pleasing others before yourself bring true fulfillment? Now that my internal moral compass has been reset, I can't believe that I could have been so naive. Make no mistake, I am not a Saint. I still get mad and lose my perspective, raising my voice to my you, my kids, and/or wife in frustration, but my patience level has gone from a 5 to an 8 on as scale of 1 to 10, and it gets better every day. And in this change of heart and attitude, (which again, was not initiated by me), I see that with this greater patience comes with it greater understanding and empathy. This change in perspective has brought about the warm and fuzzy feeling that one might think but it also carries unsettling questions as well.

I am now having a hard time understanding how it is that our society, seemingly as a whole, has decided that parenting has devolved into a burdensome reality. So-called "self-help" magazines and books invent ways to reduce and get away from the "stress" created from raising children. What kind of perspective is being sold here and, more importantly, why? Do we really need a "date night" so we can have a few hours to pretend that we are single again? And what happens once the clock tells us to go back to our self imposed "stress filled" reality? Have we really done anything to help the situation? And isn't it all really just how we picture it in the first place? Is this "getting a break" from the "rigors" of parenting creating a mindset that these breaks from our parenting "duties" allow us to survive until the next one? Did we get enough air so that we can breath for another month or so? I think there are a few million parents in this tormented world that might say that we Americans have it pretty darn good as parents. In fact, I would bet that there are quite a few mothers and fathers here in America that would give anything to have just one more minute with their child that they will never again be able to hold.

To me this is a classic case of "you don't know what you have until it's gone" and we are being told that it's okay to be so near-sighted. It's not only justifiable, but only right to take our greatest gift from God for granted so much that we need to create socially acceptable ways to avoid them.

Not me. No thanks. I will choose to love every minute that God has given me with my children not knowing how many more moments I will have.

I can understand how this may be misconstrued by those who can't see, I was once one of those people. I can also understand the welcoming of a night out with your significant other. I just think that we should make it a night of strategy, not a "much needed break" from my children and their needs.

Sure some may say what's the difference? I'm merely changing the words, but it's the same thing, and indeed it is. But the power of words is nothing short of profound as they relate to one's psychological outlook. How you talk to yourself dictates your attitude and truly is everything.

To see these one-on-one dinners as an opportunity to create a new strategy for the parenting landscape to place the importance where it belongs--- on your ability to better raise your children, not on your own selfishly made reality of needing to forget about it all for a few hours.

Now get this straight, six months ago I would have told the person writing this to 'mind your own business!', (in a less polite way), but that was before I knew what God wants from us, which is to love Him and one another with all of our hearts, souls and minds.

Upon reading the Bible from front to back and dwelling in several areas I have come to this profound understanding about our existence in the eyes of God. Now, I wonder why loving one another has become so hard?

To a small degree I have a greater understanding of the frustration that Jesus must have felt when he called us an evil generation. I often wonder what He thinks of about this cultural notion that raising children is a strenuous exercise that merely require love and guidance!

And if parenting is so taxing then why do we choose to have children? Wasn't it for love? So what's the real answer?

It's simple, Love. Love your children as if it's the last day you will be with them. When things get challenging, somehow, force yourself to remember that God will never give you more then you can handle for he knows your heart better than you do.

Remember that our children are in essence being borrowed from our Father who created them.

Have faith that you are a part of a much greater plan that only God understands, and know that it is right and necessary.

And when all else fails remember that you yourself are a child to a God who would never let you down so long as you believe these things, and love.

I truly believe that if you want to feel God's love, just hug your child in love, and there He will be.

12

STILL FREAKING OUT....a little

Hello my love. It is October 31st 2014, a little over six months since my spiritual awakening began, and I still haven't met anyone that has had a similar experience with God suddenly taking charge of their life. Thus the mystery of 'why do I deserve this miracle?' and 'is there anyone out there like me?' continues to swirl in my mind.

One thing that I know for a fact is that the change wasn't gradual because no one thing or person convinced me with words or in any other way. There was no "convincing" to it at all, I only recall suddenly knowing that God is real and has chosen me, individually, to know this wholeheartedly.

In trying to figure it out I can only recall wanting to know more about Jesus and his life, and somewhere within that phase, all doubt was removed from my being and my new life began. I know this because it was such an obvious change that I had to tell my wife about it. All doubt was removed and that changed everything else.

This newly inserted knowledge was the catalyst that set the wheels in motion. Beyond that the only thing that I can say for certain is that I have utterly fallen in love with God. A love stronger and more palpable than any I have felt since falling in love with Heidi.

It has also dawned on me that I don't love him and worship Him to gain his favor, I do this because I have gained his favor. Worship now just comes out of me most all of the time and when it isn't, I am not long from it.

In my search for someone like me I have

encountered those who obviously and truly believe in God, and in no way do I discount them or their faith, but it does little to resolve my issue of loneliness.

Don't get me wrong, it's very fulfilling to be present with other believers, and in fact it is when I am with these people of unwavering faith that I feel most comfortable. I just crave meeting someone like me.

Then again maybe they're out there but are justifiably fearful to talk about it, after all, it is a pretty confounding thing to go through. It's the suddenness of the complete conversion that really threw me for a loop and it would be completely understandable for anyone to internalize it and hide it until better understood.

I remember in vivid terms the amazement and confusion that created an excitement in me. Why would it be any different for anyone else? As a matter of fact, as I've stated before, my first reaction to it was that I was being prepared for death, that is how much it threw me off balance. I thought for a while I was certainly headed for the end. Now I think otherwise, still unsure, but I don't dwell because I no longer fear it. And after all, only God really knows so, like every other aspect of my of my life, I simply give it to Him. Unlike before this all began, I merely live each day as if it were my last.

Yeah, if they're hiding, I understand.

I have halfheartedly looked online on a desperate night or two and found accounts of people that say they have received the Holy Spirit, but not one account of having received it just out of the blue.

Researching the internet has actually been something that I have avoided simply because you just never know what you'll see in there that's actually the truth. I see plenty of those that have sought out the Spirit and claim to have received it, but wading through it is just that, WADING through it.

Living with this gift can be so lonely sometimes.

Then there's the question of what I would even do if I did find another story like mine? Do I then begin the arduous research task of finding out how to contact them? And wouldn't that be stalking? I mean, how crazy would it seem if a complete stranger called or contacted me asking personal questions about my faith? How would I respond? How would any rational person react to that? I suppose my initial reaction would be disbelief and skepticism.

No, the internet isn't the answer.

I know there must be others, just by the law of probability.

As you know, I harbor a strong desire to share my story with others. This knowledge of His realness that is so incredible to me isn't the same for those who I tell it to though. I didn't anticipate this. The reception hasn't been embraced quite like I thought it would be. I thought I was going to "change the world" for those willing to listen, just as it has changed for me. Instead the road has been wrought with pitfalls both large and small, one of which is comes all too naturally to both non-believers and believers alike.

My story sharing experiences have led me to believe that at the heart of the problem is the automatic reaction people naturally have, that there is a question of the hidden agenda.

There is a certain amount of credence that

must be given to the nature of the beast. The bare fact is most people in our culture, (and maybe all around the world), think there is always a hidden agenda.....that I am telling my story for personal gain in one way or another.

I get the feeling that people often think that maybe I'm telling my "tale" so as to paint myself up as someone special or chosen. Or possibly I'm perceived as someone trying to inspire them to become more devout in their faith so as to somehow benefit me? The fact is, I'm not! In my eyes I don't see that I'm trying to convince anyone of anything.

Each and every time I try to tell my account, my first and foremost focus is to do it with complete transparency and as it happened to its precise exactness. I sit in complete awe of everything that my spiritual awakening has done for me and I wish it to have the same effect on the listener. From how it has taken away any and all fear, to the simple elation and love that I feel all the time for which I have no explanation. I genuinely want others to feel it.

I tell my story because I feel a need to share a message of hope with the incredible desire to somehow pass the extraordinary rebirth on, nothing more, nothing less.

No, I don't have a hidden agenda for personal gain but I guess the reality is that I do have an agenda. My agenda is not so hidden though. I simply want to pass this same gift on to all, especially you my child.

I want everyone to have what I have been given because I know that having an honestly wholehearted, unshakable belief and love for God is where it all has to start. You see, there is one ultimate truth that has recently surfaced and made itself absolutely plain to me and that is that my choice to believe or not to believe must have been taken away by God. I feel as though He vaporized it from my heart in a wisp of smoke.

I look back and know that it must have been Him that took it because my about face happened so suddenly and without prompting. When I say 'about face' I don't mean that my behaviors took a miraculous turnaround, that change has been more of an evolution.

What I mean is my belief in and love for God all at once permeated my soul in a way that I've always longed for but, for whatever reason, just couldn't achieve on my own.

I have always tried to wholeheartedly believe in God but simply couldn't, (due to a lack of proof I guess). Now that I no longer need proof is completely miraculous to me. He took my doubt away and I don't know why! I guess that this is what I want everyone to understand. He simply took the doubt about His existence away, praise be to Him, not me.

The simple fact is that I have nothing to gain by explaining or convincing anyone concerning my love-filled, spontaneous life alteration. My gift has already been received, what more could I need?

The good news here is for you to know that it really happened and, apparently, it can happen to anyone at anytime. You don't have t be struggling through life, you need only BELIEVE!

I'm becoming more and more aware that when I do speak to others with whom I've already shared my story, their reactions and their expressions send a message they are becoming tired of hearing more about it. This frustrates me because I have such a great urge and need to talk about my experience that screams at me that GOD IS REAL!

It is so profoundly amazing to me, but I don't think anyone that I trust enough to tell it to wants to hear about it anymore, and frankly, I can't say that I blame them. I mean really, what should I really expect as a reaction? Can anyone really do or say anything to alleviate my compulsiveness? I recall once being the skeptical listener on the other side of the conversation and I know I would have a hard time believing it as well. After all, we've been trained since childhood to never be gullible and so I figure this probably plays a part as well.

I also ,know with my previous mentality, after hearing the story more than once I would see it as bragging, which I am most certainly not. I'm merely trying to understand what's going on.

I can't blame anyone for wishing that I would move on and quit trying to figure it out. I have in fact said just that to myself more than once....but for some reason I can't. And so, ultimately the other side of me says that patience must be the answer and right now I must continue to be.

13

DO YOU BELIEVE JUST IN CASE? (I did)

I was a lukewarm christian and halfheartedly

worshiped "just in case" God is real, so if He was and I did have to stand before Him in judgment, I would at least have that going for me. Does this sound like you?

I feel so many still are this way as well because our culture trains us to be this way. Doubt and be skepticism are a must with all the capitalistic shell gaming that goes on. But I want you to know that you can rest easy because I now know that God is real and is always here.

After all is said and done I know what is happening is real because, again, I can feel it.

Before this supernatural take over I just couldn't bring myself to fully accept God as alive, but now I know He is because I feel Him inside me and I want to shout it out! It is both tangible and palpable. I want to do this not for my benefit, but to put you at ease so maybe you can live a better life. A life without fear. A life without the abnormal stress that comes with thinking that this world is our last stop.

Unfortunately I know that my mere words aren't enough as they wouldn't have been enough for me either.

I hope that those who know me, those whom I call my friends, also recall who I was and how much I loved living a less than righteous life, and in doing so realize that something real has indeed happened to me. I pray for them to be strengthened just as I have been so that we can all be together as brothers and sisters in the heavenly realm.

I want only to let everyone know that everything will be alright because regardless of our own preconceived ideas about how our lives should or shouldn't be, there is a God in heaven that is their Father as well and in Him you can rely.

I want to let them know in a way so convincing that there isn't so much as even a hint of doubt that the Bible is alive and growing daily with the addition of another of His unwritten stories.

I want all of these things to be known for no other reason than to give them, and you, the comfort that I now feel.

I now see that we are all so desperately desiring this and are actually on a secret quest for it, but are much of the time completely unaware due to our self-righteous pride.

I wish that I could somehow articulate the

truth that has been revealed to me so accurately that it would click and make a difference so that they would all know that they no longer need to doubt.

I have been given the truth, Yes God is everywhere and he loves you and he will always be there for you!

I bring good news, God loves you because we are ALL his children! We should all be rejoicing, not fighting!

Why has God opened up my heart so that I can feel his never-ending love ALL THE TIME? I DON'T KNOW! But I know that in time I will, so I will wait patiently and praise Him in the calm AND in the storms.

Sure, I still have storms, I am human. But the difference now is that I know I need only stop and pay attention to Him instead of the noise around me and the overwhelming feeling of being loved returns in all circumstances.

It is as if my eyes have been trained to be absolutely fixed on God. The only time that I am not thinking about Him or His word is when I'm engaged in a task that requires my full attention and as soon as it ends, my thoughts transfix on Him once again.

With this spontaneous new reflex I now also see God in EVERYTHING.

At the risk of sounding like a whack-job, I believe that when we accept as fact that God has his hand in EVERYTHING it is then and only then that we are set absolutely free. It is at this wholehearted realization that all things begin to flow as they should for us as human beings.

We must put away our man-made pride forever and accept that we are not in control of ANYTHING!

When this is achieved the stress level begins to drop dramatically and happiness is compounded to a level like I have never before experienced.

This happened for me once the doubt had completely left my body. I will say it again and again, this ultimate faith must be one of the keys to receiving His love in a most complete way.

This is not to say that by accepting that He is control we should ignore the rules and laws that bind this society together. Nor is it to say that "bad" things won't happen to people and their love ones, because they will. But what we see as bad will ultimately be for the best, in time.

I watched my father die an untimely death, went through a heartbreaking divorce, and most recently have been seemingly excommunicated from most of my friends, but these things aren't "bad" things. I now realize that although painful, these occurrences happened and are happening for the greater good of His children and it is this knowledge that allows me to be thankful for them all.

It may be that we need to put away our pride and let Him know that we understand this is His kingdom, not ours. That it is by His power that ALL things should be and are for His glory, and that we relinquish ALL to Him unconditionally. To have a freedom breakthrough you my child must acknowledge that He is in control...not you.

Herein lies the potential whack-job accusation.

I personally accept that God is in full control, even in the case of something as small as a wrong turn, which delays my prompt arrival at a destination. Or when every light on the route is green and I arrive early. When I say everything, I mean every big and little thing.

Who's to say that if I hadn't missed that turn

that I would have gotten in a wreck and God stirred me to miss it to avoid the accident? Or if I hadn't made all those green lights something terrible would have happened to one on God's other children? My point is this, only He knows His plan and we should accept that it is ALWAYS for the better.

Praise Him in the calms and the storms sweetheart.

The Lord, our God is as loving and nurturing as a doe to it's newborn fawn or a first time mother is to her newly born child. But He is also as determined to do what is right as a man that just sent His only son to be slaughtered for the good of the masses... just as we do when we send our children to fight for our country in the armed forces.

For God so loved the world, that He gave His only begotten Son, that whosoever believeth in Him should not perish, but have everlasting life. (John 3:16)

......but that he loved us, and sent his Son to be the propitiation for our sins. (1 John 4:10) Who gave himself for our sins, that he might deliver us from this present evil world, according to the will of God and our Father:

(Galatians   1:4)

He that spared not his own Son, but delivered him up for us...

(Romans 8:32)

If this is true we must then believe this world is one great orchestra of life and movement created by God and the things that go on in the world can only be understood by God.

This MUST be true ALL the time, not just when it is convenient.

We should also give great gravity to the fact that we simply cannot know the reason for all happenings. Whether good or bad, some things cannot be comprehended by man. Therefore do not be overwhelmed by the thought of or dismiss the possibility that God is everywhere all the time.

My hope for you my child is that with a realization that my words are true that you no longer allow yourself to be overpowered by attempting to understand His grand design. It's just too much to comprehend so we must trust in Him.

We are very simple beings in the eyes of God. Now, to walk the talk is the true challenge to those with veiled eyes, for it is the veiled that would call me a "whack-job".... a label I will proudly wear for God.

14

SOME QUESTIONS ANSWERED

God has lifted the two ever-present questions from my heart, and of course the revealing was both startling and miraculous.

Your mom and I were discussing how things were going with my God-given quest. I say 'God-given' because quite obviously to me, I didn't start this journey, He did. I know who I was before God spun my life around and it's a far cry from who I am today. Be that as it may be, God did finally answered the two main questions that were swirling around in my head since all of this began. Number one,Why me? And number 2, having seemingly been chosen, am I special? Well, He didn't answer them entirely but He did give me a discernment that put me at ease.

After our conversation wound down, your mom went to bed so I decided to read the assigned passages from our family faith formation group. If you can remember, we as a family had joined a group at our church that was developed by our intern vicar as a part of his program that he was assigned for his development as a future pastor. We as parents were asked to read a given passage on a nightly basis to our children as a part of our bedtime routine. On this night the reading was from Philippians 2 which deals with imitating Christ's humility.

To the question of whether or not I am special the answer was a resounding NO! I read the assigned passage but something prompted me to read the scripture in it's entirety, beyond the part assigned by the vicar, and that is where I found this revelation.

As followers of Christ we should, "Do nothing out of selfish ambition or vain conceit. Rather, in humility value others above yourselves, not looking to your own interests but each of you to the interests of the others."

(Philippians 2: 3,4)

I know this passage is directed towards the Philippians but I also know now that God speaks to us by directing us to His truths in the Bible. The fact that I was discussing this very question with my wife just prior to looking at the Philippians text tells me that God was speaking to me. I know it is easy to call this coincidental but the fact is there have been too many of these kinds of occurrences since all doubt was removed to label it as such any longer. I wanted to call them coincidences at first but common sense has won out.

The last part of the scripture, (Philippians 2:12,13), "continue to work out your salvation with fear and trembling, for it is God who works in you to will and to act in order to fulfill his good purpose." This tells me that it is enough to know that He is at work in me and I should not be perplexed by the question, "why me" but, instead, feel His love and let that fill me with joy and happiness.

Reading the Bible, listening for God's message and being thankful that I am a part of God's will has allowed me to leave those once troubling questions behind.

15

Answers for atheists and agnostics, (which is what I was).

There are many questions people ask about Christianity but two stand out for me in accordance with why it is that I kept God at a distance before so I want to address them for you in case you have these same doubts.

One, is God actually man-made, and 2, who is telling the truth?

I have been researching these catechisms because most of my closest friends are of the doubting variety. I've been sandwiching this research in between my personal spiritual expansion through reading the bible.

The moat between some of my friends and a

wholehearted belief in God seems to be the question of God's existence.

Was God simply created by man to control the masses? Is there really one supreme being?

There are many paths I could choose to send you on to explain how there simply must be a single great Creator but this one stands out to me at this time.

To the unbelievers that have woven this seemingly complex curtain in the name of logic, I refer you to the work of St. Anselm who, through logic, proves that there simply must be.

In Monologium on the being of God St. Anselm breaks it down for anyone who thinks logically. He gives a detailed breakdown of the obvious, which I will attempt to sum up as neatly as possible.

Everything in existence falls under some kind of label. For example, things that help you would be under the heading of "good" and things that harm you, or your cause, would be "bad". So, if many "good things" accumulate into many more "good things" and this compounding into even greater good then all of these combined might be considered "great."

As "great" is ratcheted upwards to the upper limits it is logical to assign one final heading to all of existence as the one supreme heading. In this oversimplified explanation it becomes clear that there has to be one heading that reigns supreme. Those that know Him call Him God.

As I stated earlier, St. Anselm breaks it down in much greater detail so if you are looking for a more complete and beautiful explanation I suggest searching online for St. Anselm's Monologium on the being of God .

The other question I get from those who doubt, but want to believe, is the same one that loomed large in my own logic-entrenched brain before God intervened... who is right?

Which religion or following is correct? With so many fractions and belief systems in the world who is to be believed? In fact, if this God-imposed change of my heart hadn't happened I would still be enveloped in doubt due to this question.

To answer this now I would argue that history documents that Christianity is the only religion based on literally millions of people seeing God all at once when He descended on Mt. Sinai. In contrast, all other belief systems are based on one person witnessing God and then convincing people to follow. This, in itself makes it obvious to me who is actually telling the truth.

I fully realize that this too is probably not enough for many people to convert and believe in the one true God. I also now understand the fact is, only God can lead us to Jesus, just look no further than this author.

I can only say that I believe wholeheartedly because God permeated my fabric with doubtless belief, and now I just know who is right. After all is said and done He led me to Jesus, not anyone or anything else.

This tells me all I need to know.

Once again, all praise be to God!

16

AN EVENING WITH A FRIEND

One night while still grappling with what my life had become I decided to drop by my good friend's house to tell him what was happening to me. As a child of the sixties, this former classmate is in my opinion, an opinionated, non-combative, open-minded, self-proclaimed agnostic. He is not just a friend that is willing to listen, but his loyalty and all around good nature make him irreplaceable and I treasure our discussions because of this.

I explained to him what was happening to me and he was being the great listener that I had come to love. Upon completion of my explanation of the miracle that I felt my life had become the conversation took a turn.

I was sharing with him the miracle of God's grace and His incomprehensible ability to forgive when he said to me, "so you're telling me that I can commit horrible crimes against humanity and all I have to do is repent and I will be forgiven, even though I have been a horrible person?" I, having had this very same question haunt me before my enlightenment, hesitantly responded "yes". Before I had a chance to support my answer, my friend blurted that this is "exactly the problem" that he has with Catholics and religion in general. As if he were catching me in a cleverly laid trap he proceeded to embellish on the idea of how it just didn't stand to reason how it could be that a person could just be forgiven, no matter the offense, without any repercussion whatsoever. I could see in his eyes that he was fully convinced that he had completely painting me into a corner, so I let him finalize his seemingly infallible snare before I proceeded to explain it through divine understanding. Listening is so important in a conversation and seems to be lost in this generation that seems filled with preconceived notions and this is the strength of the conversations that we have.

I countered by explaining that God knows the hearts of all. He sees the truness of the love of those who have made a commitment to Him. This kind of wholehearted and steadfast love, by its very definition leads to forgiveness. And, with this all encompassing love for God, one no longer has any desire to commit sins against Him. At the very least, this is how I now felt.

God becomes your Father that you suddenly realize has raised you since birth with an unconditional love and compassion that exceeds all human understanding. Your love for Him is then so true and laden with respect, the thought of doing anything against Him simply doesn't exist.

I then sat silently waiting for his response anticipating to see the "light come on" but unfortunately this didn't seem to make the impact I had hoped for. He looked at me with stubbornness, shook his head with doubt and said it was all just too hard to swallow. I guess I was holding out hope that by hearing in my voice the genuine amazement while telling him my story, this great friend of mine would see the light himself and begin to entertain the thought that God is real and alive. I want so badly for all of my friends to come to the same realization that has been gifted to me, but I have sadly had to arrive at the conclusion that I can't give it to them, only Father God can.

The scriptures are simply true, there truly are those who simply cannot see or hear, just as it is written first in Isaiah 6:9,10 and then in Matthew 13:15, for the heart of this people has become dull, with their ears they scarcely hear, and they have closed their eyes, otherwise they would see with their eyes, hear with their ears, and understand with their heart and return, and I would heal them.' I know this all too well because I was one of them before He took over my thoughts.

Although strangely enlightening, this scripture breaks my heart for those who have decided to reject God. But somehow, by acknowledging this, I am given peace in knowing that it is in God's hands, not mine.

When this all began several months ago I felt a need to help those around me to "get right with the Lord" so they too would one day enter the kingdom of heaven. That desire however, created a huge amount of stress in my mind. Much to my relief, God has shown me that this pursuit is not mine but His, and that my calling is to be a light by living with the humility and Love that Jesus did.

It is truly as if it is written for me in 1st Corinthians 16:13 "Be on your guard; stand firm in the faith; be courageous; be strong. Do everything in love."

17

SWALLOW YOUR PRIDE AND YOU
WILL KNOW GOD.

I HATED this statement before I *knew*

Jesus. Why? Because it implies weakness! A vulnerability that is unacceptable for someone that relied on pride as much as I did.

As an aspiring professional athlete, self-pride was and is essential to success at the upper levels. I found that a lack of confidence at any time translated to loss, and losing is simply unacceptable at any level. Therefore I saw that to bow down and swallow one's pride as the equivalent to allowing myself to be "below par", and this attitude, as I said before, is unacceptable.

So, if having no pride was what God wanted, then I was out. But the reality is, with God, having pride is indeed just as important, it just doesn't mean what I thought, and it may not mean what you think either, sweetheart.

Looking back I now see that this incorrect view that I held of what defines pride is what kept me from knowing God, so I think this may be a key so pay attention..

I recall my wall shooting up immediately

when people told me that to really let God into my heart I must "swallow my pride". Given no further explanation I thought that meant that I was to be a sad or depressed person. Now, having been given a true understanding, I know that God doesn't want that. God wants us to be filled with pride to the maximum, but with a pride that is not boastful and self-absorbing. Instead, as His children He wants us to have a pride built on being a caring, merciful and compassionate person, full of joy and passion for life... like Jesus was.

The other statement that once caused hesitation for me was that one must humble one's self to God and then bow down to him. This conjured up ideas of injury being done to my self esteem. I refused to believe this is what God really wanted for me....to be a shame-filled servant.

My pride-filled, egotistical self got in the way of committing to God. Don't let that same misunderstanding keep you deceived.

Now I realize this isn't what happens when one humbles him/herself before God. All the negativity that I envisioned that must come with lowering one's self is actually the complete opposite of what I now feel. What actually happens is an incredible transformation into a world of love, a love that I never knew existed.

In receiving God's spirit I now know that through humbling comes a greater understanding of the one true God. It is only through complete submission to the awesomeness that He embodies in this miraculous world that our hearts can then be opened.

It's difficult to fully explain in a way I feel everyone will understand. To quote the bible works for me now but because it didn't before God changed me, I know it probably won't in this case. Scriptures alone can't reveal what I feel in my heart. It is with this admission of my egotistical barriers that I say these things.

I believe that the tipping point may be for one to submit to God with all of one's mind and heart. If this can be done, then and only then will all the stress of the false reality melt away...never to return with any staying power for longer than a fleeting moment. This is how it happened for me. For some reason, we as blinded humans have difficulty letting this change take hold in an everlasting way. For whatever reason we can't fully devour the idea of letting go of our worldly pride. Maybe this is one of the meanings behind what Jesus was referring to when He said said to them in John 6:53, "Very truly I tell you, unless you eat the flesh of the Son of Man and drink his blood, you have no life in you." One cannot eat or drink something that he/she isn't completely and fully committed to.

We too quickly forget who made us and relapse into wanting to take personal credit. At least I know I did before God showed up in my life. I continually boasted to myself that I decided what I did, not God. I believed that I earned that paycheck, I cooked that dinner, I threw that perfect pitch. As a parent or mentor I believed that I was guiding my kids down the right path. But the simple fact was that God was and is the inspiration and the mentor. Remember, without Him we wouldn't even exist.

This is so simple and straightforward but it's something I looked past every second of every day when I was blind.

Perhaps it's too simple yet blatant...once accepted. Or perhaps this is all a part of His master plan. Maybe I was supposed to see right past it until now.

Whatever the reason, I think we as a society look through and forget about this almost hidden aspect of God and how He is at work every second of every day, camouflaged by love. I am reminded of the saying "His words....our hands".

We've all heard the statement that God is love. If God is love it follows that anyone who experiences love is experiencing God. Whether they comprehend or not doesn't matter, God is there. And, if The Father is love then one must also subscribe to the idea that God is also kindness, goodness, and all that is great and good as it relates to the well being of his sons and daughters of the world. So then God must be there, in all goodness at all times.

As a Christian this concept is easy enough to understand and relinquish to. What unsettles me isn't that we can't understand this fundamental, it's the fact that we lose sight of it as quickly as a shooting star fades from the night sky.

Sure, we may be religiously keen enough to remind ourselves from time to time, but nearly as quickly as we do, we again forget.

Could it be that we get caught up in our small world false realities just as our ancestors did thousands of years ago and all throughout the ages? Has our mental evolution been frozen? Is this a part of God's master plan as well?

I believe that maybe both are true.

I think it may be helpful to examine our average, everyday occurrences more closely to fully grasp the most simple and basic workings of God that I am getting at.

For instance, when a kind word is spoken to someone that is hurting, or seeing the miracle of nature/creation, or merely cooking and delivering a hot dish for those staying in a homeless shelter.

I feel it is important to first give due gravity to how I believe most people perceive how God actually does His works.

I used to believe that if God was working in someone, he or she had to be aware of it as a miraculous happening. This was my interpretation of the stories that I know of from the bible. I've since come to realize that a burning bush or talking donkey isn't always required.

Maybe God doesn't have to come in

lightening bolt fashion. Instead, couldn't it be that God actually does His work through inspiration?

"Praise be to the Lord, the God or our ancestors, who has put it into the king's heart to bring honor to the house of the Lord in Jerusalem in this way and who has extended His good favor to me before the king and his advisers and all the king's powerful officials.

Ezra 7:27

And I also ask, are we really the ones that elect our politicians to office?

Jesus states the answer to my question clearly when He says to Pilate "You would have no power over me if it were not given to you from above."

John 19:11

"Every person is to be in subjection to the governing authorities For there is no authority except from God, and those which exist are established by God."

Romans 13:1-7

So then who really elects?

And yet we refuse to believe.

To me these passages state that we are to realize that God makes the decisions, not us. It may not be the right official elected in our minds but think about this.

According to Revelations, the world doesn't go real smoothly in the end times, so maybe the wrong choice is the right choice by His standards in accordance with His plan.

The question then becomes, do we really believe the bible as the truth?

If you believe the Bible to be the truth then He does create actions and reactions in accordance with His plan- by both miraculous occurrences as well as quietly stirring people up.

These may be hard truths, but who is the servant to tell his master he is wrong?

God is indeed at work all around us and at all times, but for Him to be seen we must first choose to look.

18

BORN AGAIN DEFINED

In the book of John, chapter 3, Jesus is teaching Nicodemus, who is a member of the Jewish council, (or put more accurately, trying to teach him),about being born again. He first says to him that;

"Very truly I tell you, no one can see the kingdom of God unless they are born again."

He then goes on to explain further to Nicodemus after he ignorantly questions how it is that a man can re-enter the womb to be reborn by saying;

"Very truly I tell you, no one can enter the kingdom of God unless they are born of water and the Spirit."

Upon my first read of this scripture I thought that Jesus was merely reaffirming his point, but when I read it a second time I noticed a difference.

Jesus had changed the wording in His first statement from "see the kingdom" to "enter the kingdom" in His second profession and it struck me between the eyes. He wasn't simply saying the same thing in a different way, He was saying two very different things to Nicodemus. I believe that every word in the Bible is put there by God in it's exact place for a specific reason. There are no idle words in The Word of God.

First in His explanation "no one can see the kingdom" I believe He's actually telling the Pharisee that because he is questioning Him on this testimony this shows that he just simply cannot understand due to the fact that he hasn't received the Holy Spirit. He is one of the blinded.

Then Jesus goes on to further explain that "no one can enter the kingdom". I believe with this difference He is telling Nicodemus that unless one in fact receives the Spirit, one will not be transformed from this worldliness. I know in my case the Spirit planted the "mustard seed" and from there my transformation began. A spiritual cleansing that has lead to the death of much of my worldly life and sin and has then gradually and seamlessly filled this new void with a new life of righteousness. And of course, no one at that moment when He was speaking to Nicodemus could receive the "water of life" due to the fact that Jesus had not yet been glorified by the Father.

Upon reading this for the second time I now

realized that this is exactly what has happened to me, I had literally been "born again"! And now I can't help but wonder if this is happening for all of God's predestined children all around the world?

Any way I look at what is currently happening to me and my life I am just thankful. Thankful to be set free of fear and doubtfulness. Thankful to have this miraculous gift given to me regardless of my brokenness. Thankful to be called a servant, for this is what I have been called to do, serve. There is no more mystery or confusion about who I am or what I am supposed to do. I am a servant of God and I am being called to serve my Father, our Father, however He calls me to, and that's it.

Maybe I have been called to a more active role. What that role is has yet to be determined but to know that I have been called, no matter what the path, should further limits my confusion and to this I say a resounding AMEN!

19

ANOTHER JOURNAL ENTRY

January 25, 2015

The Spirit has re-energized me! I know this to be true because I am brimming with love and joy, just like the day that I received Him the first time- exactly the same feeling! I'm not sure why, I don't even think that I need it because I am still filled just as before with a passionate curiosity for the Bible and a joy filled sense of being. I don't really know what to make of it all but THANK YOU GOD!

20

STILL DISCERNING

What I once thought to be the filling of the Holy Spirit I now have come to realize is actually the Kingdom of God. What I mean to say is that the Holy Spirit is actually the Helper, just as Jesus said Him to be and the Kingdom is actually something entirely different.

There was a moment, a single glorious moment when the Spirit came into my life, and it was at that moment that I completely understood the sacrifice made for me personally by Jesus. When this occurred I knew for the first time in my life the true and perfect love of God and a callous was shaved off of my heart, my eyes were opened, muffles were taken off of my ears and then the kingdom began to grow. It was at this point that I think that maybe the "mustard seed" that Jesus spoke so often about was planted in me by the Helper and an insatiable appetite began to grow in my heart and mind for the word of God and the wisdom and knowledge therein.

Now it continues to flourish and grow, as does my confidence to share it with others. As I was once shy and scared to offend, I now am unafraid and proud to share with those that are willing to listen.

The Kingdom of God that Jesus describes in Mark 4:30 and Luke 13:18-21 is exactly what has taken place in me. This in itself is an amazing thing to have happen, but to have it infiltrate my heart and soul is what continues to confound me.

It was 8 yrs prior to the Arizona experience that my baptism took place, so why the delay? I know these questions may not seem that important but the fact that I didn't receive this free gift from God by means of works is. At least it is to me because it means that God in some instances chooses us, we don't choose Him. It is not what we do for Him but what He chooses to do for us. This is God's will, not ours. I've heard it explained very well in this way.

Say you are a master and you have many servants, all of whom has stolen from you in one way or another and you put them all into a room and decided to choose some over others to forgive and give an additional gift to. Would you not have the right to do this? As the master don't you have the power to do whatever pleases you? Can't you decide what is fair or acceptable?

This is what God has chosen to do. What His decision is based on is entirely up to Him, and so for the other thieves to consider the choice unjust is indeed outrageous in itself.

Children, God is always faithful and just in accordance with His plan and we must remain faithful knowing that it will always work in favor of His children. And if you trust and love and believe in Him then in the end you will be saved.

21

TRANSFORMATIONAL DIFFICULTIES

Being led by the Spirit is a tangible thing that is both easy and hard. Easy because the transformation is both welcomed and effortless, hard because it defies logic.

When I say effortless I mean that with the planting of the "mustard seed" comes the inherited will to be righteous in everything that I do. This doesn't mean that I AM righteous in everything that I do, but that I am now very grieved if I make a bad knee-jerk response.

When I say 'defies logic' I mean this. I had always been under the impression that God transformed people by first breaking them down and yet I was in a happy place in my life, just minding my own business when it all started. Also illogical is the fact that it took only a minimal effort to stop committing the habitual sins of alcoholism and drug abuse that once held me captive for so long. Once I realized that the effects of the drug was masking the awesome feeling of love on my heart that God was giving to me it was, as they say, a no-brain-er! We need only have the awesome and all powerful God take a personal interest in you. To me the fact that He did this for me is mind-boggling. I mean really, who am I?

I am His slave, that's who I am, and I love it!

Although transformation doesn't happen quickly, it really couldn't be easier due to the fact that I have no logical choice in the matter. It really is as if you are a branch of the vine that is simply being pruned so as to provide better fruit and just like the vine must feel great during the growth of the newly forming fruit, so do I!

To put it another way, it's the same feeling that you get when you fall in love for the first time. A supernatural, never felt before, deeper than deep drive to be with that person. This is what precisely happened to me over a year ago and, unlike my first, "first love" that gets weathered and old, this intense love has done nothing but grow fresher and newer over time.

But again, why me and why now? Although this ever-present question looms smaller, it does still exist, but now I think I may finally know the answer. It's for God.

Duh, right? But it isn't so obvious when it happens to YOU. You see, when it happened I was convinced that I was already an outward-looking person. Someone that could put myself in other people's shoes and understand and have empathy for whatever and whoever in all situations, but I was wrong. I was actually very inward-looking and self absorbed in my needs and wants.

I held the belief that if I wasn't pleased then how could others that I came in touch with find me pleasing? Now I know the truth and have been set free of this lie, praise God!

Now I understand the true reality and I realize that I have been transformed for you my child, to serve you. Father God has saved me for my family! I have been made a witness for anyone willing to listen, but mostly it has happened for Him,....God.

I have been given this awesome gift of grace and faith to shine it on the world for the glorification of our Father in heaven.

To inspire people to believe me was all that I could focus on at first and now I can't even care about that because I realize that whether or not you or anyone else believes isn't up to me, it's up to Him, I'm just here to shine like a light on a hill for Him. This is His will and that is simply what I MUST do.

It's like this sweetie. Father God is our creator, much like a potter creating something from clay. He is making each of us to serve His purpose and therefore who am I to judge or criticize anyone else which is His creation?

To judge is NOT our calling. His desire for us is to live a wonder-filled life and to love Him and one another as Jesus loved His disciples.

God is alive inside me and it is so much more than a feeling, it is as tangible as the chair that I'm sitting in.

I now know the excitement that Mary had when she went to Elizabeth to tell her of her experience! With the sharing of the news that they had in common, the electricity in the room must have been through the roof! This is how I felt when I felt the great news of being claimed as His son. He is now in me and I am now in Him and I have been made this new creature to proclaim it to you that He loves YOU too! Now go out and be a light for Him in this broken and dark world.

This doesn't mean that you must stand on a street corner and shout it out, (but of course you can if you feel compelled :). What you should always do is look for those that He sends to you and proclaim the gospel. Look for the doors that He will open and then walk through them with confidence that He is with you. This is the true power of the Spirit and it feels absolutely glorious!

22

SO WHO'S RIGHT ANYWAY?

Before my transformation began I, like many, thought that only one denomination or system of religious beliefs could be "the right one", but now that I have been led to Jesus, The Truth, I know better.

I now understand that to be a part of His holy church one must wholeheartedly believe in God and Jesus as the Messiah and that He was sacrificed to atone for our sins and then rose from the dead as the first fruit and is seated at the right hand of our Father in heaven. These are those who make up the body of the bride, or "church", and He, our Lord and Savior, is the head. And so, just as our bodies have many parts that make it the miracle that it is, so does the body of Christ.

So as to keep on track I suggest that you to follow this advice. Instead of letting your pride rule over your thoughts of who is right and who is wrong, let your heart be transformed and renewed as mine has been and see that this division between the different parts of the body aren't important. Come to realize as I have that to divide and conquer is the plan of Satan and do not let him have control over your mind in this or any way. Remember that this divided way of thinking can only produce evil and so it cannot be from God.

I also want you to know this fact. I see now that our God has been with me all throughout my life and He is with you as well right now. He has opened my eyes and has allowed me to see Him in everything since April of 2014. If the road to Him was through anyone or anything else He would have led me to that person or system of beliefs. Instead, He led me to Jesus!

Therefore JESUS is truly the way, just as it is

stated His original disciples.

Thomas said to Him,"Lord, we do not know where You are going, how do we know the way?" Jesus said to him, "I am the way, and the truth, and the life; no one comes to the Father but through Me.

John 14:5-6

Consider once again that I was NOT looking to become more spiritual or righteous when this occurred and so the only conclusion that I can reach is that the gift of faith and grace is truly free and does not depend on good works. It is clear to me that the way to God is NOT through works or service, these are an outpouring that occurs as a reaction.

If the belief that one must DO something to be seen in God's eyes as righteous were true then why has He done this to me? Furthermore, what did the disciples DO to be chosen?

Remember my child, God sees and knows our hearts better than we do, just as Jesus knew that Peter would betray Him, not once but three times, before the cock crowed. He sees the heart not the works. He demands mercy, not sacrifice.

No, one belief system is superior to another. God has a plan that surpasses all human understanding, so for us to toil on any of this pride-filled haggling is not what He wants. What He wants is for us to complete the task that Jesus began and that is to spread the good news, spread the gospel and make disciples.

The world today is overflowing with bad news. I believe that people want to hear, and people need to hear the good news. We need to proclaim witness to Jesus as our savior to all willing to listen, not squabble over which part of the body of Christ is better than the other.

We are to love only God with all of our hearts, souls and strength, not love ourselves and the things that we can accumulate here on earth. We are to love one another and treat each other with the same kindness that we ourselves desire.

If we would all just do these seemingly simple tasks that Jesus showed us to be humanly possible then we could ALL experience Heaven right here, right now.

I may be a simple slave, but this I know is the

end goal of His miraculous and inconceivable plan, LOVE!

Be still and know that I and He loves you.

23

RANDOM UNDERSTANDINGS

The thought of praising Father God excites me like a child about to open a Christmas present. Is this weird? Hmmmmm....

After many hours of studying God's word and living this transformation out I have come to this as my conclusion thus far.

I have been drawn to Jesus by The Father Almighty and been educated by Him. I did not seek for this to happen, it just did. I now live involuntarily nearly every moment of every hour in some sort of praise to my Father in heaven and the only time I don't is when I am actually engaged in conversation with someone about something else. But, as soon as it concludes I am immediately drawn to Him once again in some way shape or form, and I know and feel that He is all around me ALL of the time.

This metamorphosis has been truly incredible and it continues to this very moment and I pray for it to never end until the day that He comes for me.

I embrace it with all of my heart, soul and strength. I am in constant wonder and awe of how I have been blessed. The love that I feel is beyond explanation and nearly incomprehensible to me. In fact I used to be afraid to even talk about it for fear of having it taken away for being boastful. Now I know that God's love is never ending to His children so I fear no more, nor do I boast.

The simple fact is this....Jesus has taken up residency in me and the same Spirit that raised Him from the dead lives in me. How awesome is that!

24

P salm 23 through my new eyes

(How it reads to me)

The Lord is my shepherd; I shall not want.

(God guides me and because He has given me all that I need, what more is there to want?)

He maketh me to lie down in green pastures;

He leadeth me beside still waters.

(*God has taken me by the hand and this comforts me and has rid me of all worries and fears.*)

He leadeth me in the path of righteousness for His name's sake.

(*My Father has taken me by the hand and is guiding me away from the path of sin and down a sinless one that I didn't know existed.*)

Yea though I walk through the valley of the shadow of death, I will fear no evil: For thou art with me; Thy rod and staff they comfort me.

(*No matter what I may face here on earth I will have no real fear because I know now that you now and always have been with me; Father your guidance and discipline give me peace and love.*)

Thou preparest a table before me in the presence of mine enemies; Thou anointest my head with oil; my cup runneth over.

(*Although I may experience hard times here on earth I know I have a place at your table in heaven; You have given me your free gift of grace and I want only to spill it on all those you lead me to, so I will.*)

Surely goodness and mercy shall follow me all the days of my life; and I will dwell in the house of the Lord forever.

(*No matter the circumstance I've known that from the day you poured out your Spirit on me to the end of my time here on earth ALL will be for the good and merciful toward me for I know it to be your will and so I will accept it joyfully; and I will be with You, The Holy Spirit and my Lord and Savior Jesus Christ in heaven one fine day.*)

AMEN.

THIS I KNOW AS TRUTH...I HOPE THAT
YOU CAN KNOW IT AS WELL;

An enduring inner peace is obtained when one can
wholeheartedly submit to the understanding that God
is in control, not us.

25

HIS LOVE STARTS WITH YOUR LOVE

I want so badly to give what give you what

has been given to me so I continue to try and figure

out how to do that. In contemplating this seemingly

impossible feat I seem to gravitate to one thing, true love.

You say that you love Jesus but do you really LOVE Him? I ask this question because I know that I used to think that I loved Him the most but in actuality, I did not. I loved myself more.

I wanted to love Him the most, that wasn't the problem, I just didn't take the time to know Him well enough to really LOVE Him more than anything else, and this is what it takes.

When I actually fell in true love with Jesus it happened when I took the time to totally internalize what it is that He did for me and so I suggest this. Take the time to research what His life was really like. It's an incredibly important journey and story.

I look back and I think it was while watching the motion picture depicting His passion for His children that I really fell into Love with Jesus Christ. I didn't really know it at the time. In fact it wasn't until later that I realized what had happened.

At the viewing of the Mel Gibson directed movie Passion Of The Christ I felt nearly overwhelmingly sad. It wasn't actually until after the movie had ended that I recall my respect for Him deepening to the point of love. I remember I wanted to both cry and laugh at the same time.

This leading of me by The Father to Jesus then in turn led me to The Father. This is when God showed me His incredible love in His heart for me personally, through the scriptures. This is what has happened to me and I believe that this is where it has to start.

We must first fall in love with Jesus and then keep His commands, but to keep His commands you have to really fall in love with Him then it is easy.

This was brought to my attention most pointedly when I read John 14:24, "Anyone who does not love me will not obey my teaching. These words you hear are not my own; they belong to the Father who sent me."

This then is the test. Do you always obey His teachings? Do you really love Jesus?

This love that I am talking about is nothing short of supernatural. It is not something that I could have achieved on my own. Quite simply, it just came to me, praise be to God. But I also know this from the teaching in the gospel of Luke, chapter 11, verses 10-13;

"For everyone who asks receives; he who seeks finds; and to him who knocks, the door will be opened.

What father among you, if his son asks for a fish, will give him a snake instead?

Or if he asks for an egg, will give him a scorpion?

If you then, though you are evil, know how to give good gifts to your children, how much more will your Father in heaven give the Holy Spirit to those who ask him!"

Please, continue to seek out His heart, you won't regret it my child.

KNOW THIS TRUTH

We are not called to judge. We are not called to boast. We are not called to exalt men or be exalted by man. We are called to be transformed and speak the gospel. Tell others what The Great Creator has done for you out of His grace and mercy. Do not concern yourself with how others should live. We are called to be a light in the darkness and to live with the passion of Christ.

Lead with your actions, for only Jesus can save. Be transformed by the Helper that has been given to you. Open yourself to Him so that you may be cleansed of your inherited sinful nature and concern yourself with nothing else. To engage in anything other than listening for, and expelling the demons that are attempting to deceive you is allowing yourself to be tricked and delayed. He is extending His arms open wide to you, run into them!

Remain focused on the spiritual realm for this is where you belong, not in the flesh. To be caught up in challenging others and their interpretations of what you know to be true is to allow yourself to be further delayed.

Remember this, we cannot be pleasing to Him in the flesh. Live in the Spirit. Do not be deceived or postponed any longer. Open up to the Comforter gifted to you on every opportunity and be cleansed. Take authority over all unclean spirits, as this ability was given to you by Jesus Christ. Be God's child, not of the flesh but of the spirit.

Live as our Father intended us to live when He first raised us from the dust. Live life fully and without fear, for if God is for us then who can be against?

Fear not and live in peace.

26

How to truly forgive

H ow can one forgive the fact that a person has stolen something of great value from them, or has done them a deeply felt wrong? How can one truly forgive someone?

True forgiveness can only be had from God if we first forgive those who have sinned against us. We as Christians have been taught this by Jesus from understanding the Lord's prayer, "and forgive us of our sins as we forgive those who have sinned against us"....so how do we forgive truly and wholeheartedly someone?

Because God has a plan and that it is truly inconceivable to man. I also know that it must simply be accepted, so I do. In this acceptance I also realize that whatever part I play in it, I must also accept that as well, both in the calm and the storm. So with this in mind I know that what I may perceive as "bad" is actually for the better for God's children, as is stated in Romans 8:28 "And we know that all things work together for good to those who love God". So, in keeping this at the forefront, I know that whatever has happened to me has been

God's will, and in knowing this, I am thankful for whatever He has gifted me with, both "good" and "bad". With this knowledge how then can I not forgive? Here's an example from my life.

I lost my first family through a painful divorce many years ago. At the time I, and my dream of how my life was going to be, was shattered. I barely ate or slept for two weeks. It seemed unfair and I suffered immensely. But, I am now in another even more miraculous dream that I had no idea even existed. Father God had a plan for me that was beyond my ability to comprehend at that time and His plan was to make beauty from my sufferings. I simply could not have understood it from the vantage of my position at the time.

From that experience I know now that trying to understand and therefore predict God's will is foolish, so I now just accept it, and in doing so, how can I not forgive those who have sinned against me? They were an integral part of the plan for me to be in this miracle that I now live in. I am actually thankful for what they have done as I now see that if it weren't for what happened at that time, I wouldn't be in this wonderful life that I have today.

Maybe now you can look back on your journey and see where this may be true for you as well. Also, I hope you can take heart in knowing this. If you are in a less-than-desirable place today, stay calm, because much, MUCH better is in your future as long as you take the high road, love and pray.

27

WHO ARE YOU?

My child, our Father in heaven continues to give me revelations and I hope that I relay this, and all of them, in a way that you can fully comprehend so that you can better understand both me and maybe even yourself.

As I continue to search God's heart for guidance and answers, the questions that once boiled continuously, (why have you changed ME God...and why now?), have been slid to the back burner and reduced to low. Given the miracle that my life has become, more than anything I am just thankful to feel His love so vividly. Those questions, now more superficial than ever, just aren't as important anymore. I am also acutely aware that this is His story and His will, not mine, so I should just be content knowing I am His now and forever.

But they do, however, remain on *A* burner, simmering away. And so I continue to seek, and in my quest for answers I have come to yet another understanding that I know is important so I want to share it with you. But I also feel it's important to set the stage once again.

To rekindle let's take a step back in time for a moment. I want you to try and put yourself in my shoes back in 2014.

You have a beautiful family and you have no financial worry. You aren't wealthy but you are debt free. Everyone in your family is doing well and you are enjoying your life. Then, all of a sudden, out of nowhere, God decides to redo who you are from the inside out. And when I say redo, I mean a sudden and complete metamorphosis from a liberally thinking party animal to a completely dedicated disciple of Jesus.

Although strange enough all by itself, here's the kicker, YOU DIDN'T ASK FOR IT! Now take a moment or two and chew on that. Metaphorically speaking, I went from being an apple to an orange virtually overnight!

No, don't move on, really try and put yourself

in my shoes and think about this for a minute.

This new reality is what I am still fully immersed in today, October 15th, 2016, but things have changed a bit. I have finally been given some answers and I am now compelled to write them to you with the hope that they may help you know God to a greater degree. They are not the answers to those questions of "why me or why now", but an answer to satisfy another constant inquiry in my heart and that is this; what do you want me to do now that I know I'm your child? Where do I fit into your plan?

I know our Creator tells us in many of His writings through His bond servant the Apostle Paul that we are all being changed into the image of His son. I get that, but what is my role? What does He want me to do now that I am clothed in His Armour?

And so I continue to love to pray and dig into His word for answers because it is here that I find my greatest peace.

One particular night, a few weeks back, I was searching out His heart through the gospel of John. I had read this book of gospel several times but when I examined it this time around, something new stood out. A whole new dimension shone brightly in the 17th chapter and an indisputable fact laid there before me that I hadn't realized before.

In this glimpse through God's word into the prayer life of Jesus, He is about to be crucified and so He prays what has been called the Farewell prayer or the High priestly prayer.

In this prayer spoken by Jesus He asks for three blessings.

1. Glorify Him/Jesus, so that He may glorify God by giving all those that God has given to Him eternal life.

2. Secondly Jesus prays for His disciples, those that God has given to Him- the elected predestined children.

3. Then, lastly Jesus prays for those who believe in Him through His disciples testimony.

In my past readings I had always got caught up in *what it is* that Jesus is praying for, not *who* He is praying for. This time it was different. I recall looking at these passages of scripture and wanting to re-read it rather than moving on, so I did, And there it was!

There are those who were chosen by God and those that, **by their own free will**, choose to believe.

There are categories of the saved!

So what does this mean?

When Jesus was praying for His disciples, I believe He was not just praying only for the disciples of that time, no, He has a plan. A plan that spans all time. Of course He knew that people would be reading the bible many years into the future, and so of course Jesus prayed this prayer for us as well. This part of the prayer was for His present AND FUTURE disciples. And because of what has happened to me, I believe that this is where I fit in. I am a predestined disciple. How do I know this to be true?

Take into account the fact that I rose from my slumber one morning and suddenly became overwhelmingly curious for Jesus. This tells me that I was led to Jesus, plain and simple. I didn't choose Him, He chose me. The fact of the matter is, I must then be a predestined disciple. This I already knew but what suddenly dawned on me is the fact that He said that they, (the disciples) are not of the world just as He is not of the world. Couple this with Paul's many writings but more specifically…..

And we know that God causes all things to work together for good to those who love God, to those who are called according to His purpose. For those whom He foreknew, He also predestined to become conformed to the image of His Son, so that He would be the firstborn among many brethren; and these whom He predestined, He also called; and these whom He called, He also justified; and these whom He justified, He also glorified.

Romans 8:28

I had literally been given to Jesus on that morning that I suddenly became hungry for Him. And I wasn't just hungry, I was suddenly starving! And then later, God's word! And I reiterate, I didn't feel that I had a choice, praise be to God! I was chosen by God before the beginning! I am one of these that God foreknew to be His as a part of His great and unimaginable plan.

Although you may assume that in comprehending this I therefore believe that I am special, or superior, I don't. Why? The fact remains that on my own I couldn't wholeheartedly believe to the degree necessary to activate the Spirit. I didn't do this, He did. I'm not special. Those who can believe of their own free will, they are the special ones. Even as Jesus washed the feet of His disciples, so must I wash theirs. **I am now His servant, a slave for our Father, the one true God.**

Now let's move on, because the real eye opener is yet to come.

The next part of His prayer is the really incredible part because in there He reveals the rich and wonderful grace of our incredibly merciful God.

After this second part of His prayer to God, Jesus goes on to pray for those that believe in Him through the message of His disciples.

Here Jesus prays for the blessed believers that remain free to choose.

Our savior prays for the Holy Spirit to also be poured out to those who choose of their own free will to believe so that they may know Him, (God) and be one with Him just as He, (Jesus), was.

These are the truly blessed! Those who choose to believe without having to see.

How do we know that these are the "blessed"? We know this by what Jesus tells Thomas in John 20;29 "blessed, are those who have not seen and yet have believed".

This is something that I simply could not do and I am continually humbled by those who can.

There are two categories of saved children, those who were chosen by God and those that choose to believe. So how do you know which division you are in?

Ask yourself this, Do you know and love God? And when I say "know" Him I mean, not just to know about Him but to actually feel Him inside you as a real entity. I mean do you know Him just as you know me and my real existence?

If you don't feel Him inside you then you must choose to believe…. and then you will.

And so I give you this revelation.

Maybe YOU are the blessed! One that can believe without having to see. Maybe this is where you fit in. Or maybe you have had what has happened to me, happen to you and you are a slave for God as well. Either one will do. Just BE ONE.

But in case you are still not sure what to make of all of this, know this…

I know it was when I truly and wholeheartedly believed that everything began to change for me.

Now the rest is easy. My yoke has truly been made light. Being right with God has become instinctual, not burdensome. And so it can be for you. You need only believe and ask for Him to come into your heart to lead you, He will take care of the rest!

Just do this my love, ***believe***, for He is real.

28

AND SO TO SUMMARIZE...

I began this journal to try and make sense of what was suddenly happening to me from the inside out and at this point, two and a half years later, this much I know to be true.

FACT:

I have been changed both physically and

mentally.

My taste in everything has changed for the better and I am much more emotionally invested in everything more than ever before. My outlook on life and people have gone from being inward in nature and self pleasing, (which I didn't realize), to one of pleasing God first in everything I do.

FACT:

I did not ask for this change.

Do you understand what this must mean? I have either blown a fuse and for reasons unknown cannot get enough of God and His words,.... or God has done this and so therefor **HE IS REAL!**

I know the truth and have therefor been set free, and this is my prayer for you as well.

FACT:

We are in the end times.

What part of the end, I, nor anyone else can tell you with absolute certainty, but I know this, we aren't in the beginning, that was many, many years ago. So then we must then be somewhere toward the end part, and from the looks of the state of humanity not too far away from the new beginning.

QUESTION:

If Jesus came today, ARE YOU READY?

If you aren't sure then all you have to do is believe in Him, commit to Him and pray for Him to lead your life as your Lord and Savior. Do this and you will undoubtedly be ready.

I love you and so does God the Father of us all.

29

CLOSING PRAYER (*for you and me*)

As a parent I can only wish for my children to have happiness and fulfillment in life. You too will feel this way if you don't already, and so my child, I hope you pray and live by the Lord's prayer **as it is written**.

Also remember this. When you do anything difficult, always look to Jesus and remember His undisturbed face and this will tell you to be undisturbed as well.

These are my final words to you.

Know at all times that you are a child of God's. Never let the thoughts of doubt creep in because that is how times of trouble begin. Just as Jesus was tempted in the wilderness so too are we each and every day in multiple ways. Notice though, in all of the temptations that Satan tries to use against our Lord they begin with him trying to create doubt in Jesus' mind. Doubt about who He is.

The devil said to him, "If you are the Son of God, tell this stone to become bread."

Luke 4:3

We too must rebuke the Deceiver sternly and remember who we are, just as He did! This is the example being set in this scripture.

And lastly, but of course never the least, ALWAYS put God first, loving Him with all your heart, soul, mind and strength.

When times of trouble are upon you, pray to

Him. When times of joy are upon your life, pray to Him.

In doing this you will always be an outflow of love.

My final prayer;

Father God I pray that you give me the wisdom to always recognize that everything is your will, just as Jesus tells His disciples when He tells them how to pray, ("Your kingdom come, _**Your will be done on earth as in heaven**_"), so that I may accept and embrace whatever circumstance and serve you fully and therefore glorify your name in everything I do. And so with this knowledge I also pray that I am continuously thankful for each and every occurrence that happens both around me and to me, for I know that it is Your plan not mine and therefore always for the greater good for your children.

Amen.

ONE LAST
ACKNOWLEDGMENT

All of what you have read were the writings during a time when I was being taught strictly by God. I did not wake up one day and decide to begin to study the bible so that I could puff myself up, and I have never done any study of God or His word to *knowingly become anything.* I have struggled with the idea of selling this work but have concluded that if it leads someone to Him then maybe this was God's intention. And you should know that all monies gained from becoming a part of His story will go right back to Him and spreading the gospel because if it weren't for Father God doing this to me in the first place I wouldn't have anything worth writing about.

PRAISE GOD FOR HE IS WORTHY!

A FINAL THANK YOU

I have been blessed to have been given to an incredible and strong and loving family. Thank you so much Mom, Dad, John, Dee Dee, and Mike. You have been an absolutely unshakable foundation on which God has put me and for that I am grateful beyond words.

www.ingramcontent.com/pod-product-compliance
Lightning Source LLC
Chambersburg PA
CBHW071419040426

42331CB00050B/2529